Historic Tales
of the
HIAWATHA
VALLEY

Historic Tales

of the

HIAWATHA VALLEY

KENT OTTO STEVER, PhD

THE
History
PRESS

Published by The History Press
Charleston, SC
www.historypress.com

Copyright © 2019 by Kent Otto Stever
All rights reserved

First published 2019

Manufactured in the United States

ISBN 9781467143097

Library of Congress Control Number: 2019936996

Contents

Introduction

The [Mississippi] *river is a moving, living, changing thing.*
Its path matches the route of the glaciers in the manner of a pygmy walking
the path of giants. The river has been in this valley for perhaps 250 million
years. When the seas retreated, there lay warm, carboniferous swamps, tall with
great fern trees and moss clumps as big as oak trees.
By road or boat, a journey along the modern Mississippi is an adventure. The
sandstone bluffs that mark the horizon in all directions look down upon a marriage
of busy commerce and ancient lore. The same stream that long ago carried the
log rafts and paddle-wheelers today carries towboats that strain thousands of
horsepower against barge tows of more than three football fields in length.

—*Arlen Albrecht,* Minnesota Volunteer, *May/June 1973*

With Mississippi River lore, a natural beauty and the history of a Native American culture as base roots, the Hiawatha Valley of southern Minnesota has become a tourist mecca. Also known as Hiawathaland, this unofficially named valley of nearly one hundred miles has scenery rivaling that of the Danube, Rhein and Moselle River Valleys of Europe. It is often called "Little Switzerland."

Hills and valleys that surround the river are home to some of America's most beautiful farms and top dairy herds. Observing Caledonia's deep valleys in the south or the 450-foot bluff tops interspersed along the Mississippi from Dresbach to Red Wing—one wants to yodel.

While viewing this expansive area and observing the approach of ensuing glaciers that threatened to bulldoze the future lands of Red Wing and Hastings of the north; Winona, LaCrosse, LaCrescent and Trempealeau of the south; and all the villages in between, God said, "Stop! This is my land!" He recognized that the buildup of strata of sand and gravel as glaciers pushed through in their distinct periods of glacial and fluvial action was to form unique and distinctive shapes. Three-hundred-foot bluffs on either side of the Mississippi for nearly one hundred miles, beginning from the Mississippi's confluence with two other rivers at LaCrosse and expanding upriver well beyond Red Wing, have been saved for the generations.

God's surround has thus become a valley of history—a wooded valley surrounded by rich upland plains. The home to buffalo driven off the bluffside by Native Americans dating back centuries in time, it became the official home of the Sioux with the Treaty of 1830 declaring it their home.

"The Song of Hiawatha" by Henry Wadsworth Longfellow in 1855 gave rise to the informal naming of Hiawatha Valley. Hiawatha, depicted by Longfellow, is the son of the West Wind. His name is derived from an Iroquois word meaning "he makes rivers." Overcoming evil forces, Hiawatha offers "the gift of civilization to the world." His marriage to Minnehaha leads to "a golden age of happiness and peace."

Those who have lived their lives in this valley understand that happiness and peace. They have driven their cars up and down their portion of the two-lane, river-hugging Highway 61 from Red Wing to LaCrescent, a part of a well-known national roadway that travels from Canada to the Gulf of Mexico. Early settlers attended the Sunday afternoon baseball games of the Hiawatha Valley League at Rollingstone, St. Charles, Lewiston, Chatfield, La Crescent and Alma. Today's school leagues and the Hiawatha Educational District of the region extend the valley's boundaries even farther westward to encompass small towns of the Rochester area.

In the 1930s, communities and representatives from LaCrosse, Winona, Wabasha, Lake City, Red Wing and Hastings banded together to form the Hiawatha Valley Association, a volunteer custodial organization that promoted the valley's virtues, people and hospitality. Thousands of brochures and descriptions were distributed annually throughout the state and region. Like the Arrowhead and Paul Bunyan tourist regions of northern Minnesota, the Hiawatha Valley today offers a unique heritage and set of homilies, recipes, nationalities, traditions and heritage to be shared.

At the "gateway" to the valley, and to its bluffland and prairie plains, is the city of Winona. It has been "heart and center" to the region's

Winona Bridge. Steve Deeren photo, used with permission. *Author's collection.*

growth. Conversion from the nation's first and largest lumber and flour milling operation of the nineteenth century through the bustling era of steamships, railroads and agriculture has led Winona to today's cultural and industrial leadership, all while standing steadfast as a leading protector of God's great valley.

Winona's worldwide leadership in household products of the past one hundred years was established by the J.R. Watkins Company. That leadership continues with Watkins today and with the $5 billion of annual sales of construction fasteners by Fastenal of Winona, created on Second Street. The nearly one thousand furniture outlets of Ashley of Arcadia, Wisconsin serve internationally. Each has grown outward from the Hiawatha Valley and the people therein. In the beauty of its natural surround of hills, river and lake, the fame of the valley and Winona is reaching around the world.

Passing the distinctive Sugar Loaf (or Wah-Pa-Sha's Cap) of Winona, where Lieutenant Zebulon Pike first observed the valley in 1805, one is led north on a winding path to the pristine beauty of Lake City and Lake Pepin. There, a similar outcropping faces across the lake from Diamond

Bluff, Wisconsin, to mark the resting place of the Maiden Wee-no-nah, distraught first daughter of Chief Wah-Pa-Sha of the Sioux tribe. In the place of her alleged freefall death from the bluff, there is a surround of beauty in all seasons.

Chimney Rock, Bald Bluff, Reed's Landing, Wabasha, Pepin and Alma (Wisconsin) are all sites near the historic village of Minneska, Minnesota (today's Minnieska at the juncture of the Mississippi and the White Water Rivers) that surround the river's southern approach to the grand entrance to Lake Pepin—a majestic, twenty-two-mile lake formed by the "scooping out" of the earth by a huge descending glacial hill that pushed from northwest to southeast.

The stories that follow encapsulate the history and the spirit of the valley and its people. Through well-researched, documented and real experiences evidenced by a one-hundred-year historical newspaper database, the author presents the real case of a marvelous people, as well as achievements and places that still fill his bones as "home." Little essays and vignettes created of those times offer some of the author's personal experiences relating to those very real people. A special story of Wee-no-nah sets the stage for entry into the valley.

Artist unknown, a 1900s original painting hung for years in the "front room" of the author's small family home on Grand Street in Winona. To the six kids of that household, the painting was magical—relating directly to their beautiful river valley, to the Native American culture surrounding them and to the fabled story of Wee-no-nah, for whom the city of Winona was named. After fifty years of pondering, the author decided to create a story to help define the painting. (Note: The painting follows at end of that story.)

Although raised with the supposed tale of Wee-no-nah, he had not read a printed version of the story until he ventured across Major Long's 1899 report from an expedition of 1823—after he had completed the story here. It has been suggested by the Winona Historical Society that fifty stories and versions of Winona exist. The original painting remains with the author today.

The author, a Winona native, lived some of the history—enjoying thousands of hours outdoors in all seasons of God's great world. It has been said by another that his offerings might be likened to "love stories" of one who grew up in the beautiful valley's great surround. As he traveled the river valley one recent summer's night, his heart was again renewed.

He thanks you for joining him on the journey.

Love in the Prairie Grass

WEE-NO-NAH'S STORY

Morning Star, a young Wahpeton Sioux brave, lived in a valley of sunshine and happiness along the Great River. The love of his life was Wee-no-nah, the sparkle-faced firstborn daughter of Chief Wah-Pa-Sha, leader of the Dakota band of Native Americans inhabiting lands from Prairie Du Chien north to Red Wing—a distance of more than seventy-five miles along the Great River.

On sand prairie, in woods or on water, Morning Star excelled. He crisscrossed deer trails in the woods and fished the river. His father, Waditaka, the Courageous One, gave him a birch-bark canoe made from the trees of the forest at the age of seven.

His water ventures began on a small lake formed by a divergence of the Great River. It was a safe place—away from the current and dangers of the big river. Daily he tested his canoeing and fishing skills in the tanpawata. By the age of ten, Morning Star was guiding other young Indians onto the lake and into the backwaters of the river.

His catch of fish easily supplied his family's needs over the warm months. When autumn came, he joined his father and others in gathering larger and more numerous fish to be smoked over the campfire and held for winter sustenance.

Morning Star grew up with Wee-no-nah in their small village on the sand prairie, an area formed a millennium ago by retreating icebergs sculpting a river, bluffs and valleys. From spring breakup of ice on the lake and river through coldest days of winter, they were together for sojourns by water and

Village of Keoxa/Wapasha's Prairie, early Winona. Plate 22. *H. Lewis. Courtesy Winona History Center.*

land travel across valleys, creeks and hillsides. They fished and swam and hunted and climbed.

The young man and his beautiful friend's travels ranged within the several miles of their sand prairie village on Wah-Pa-Sha's Prairie, a flat sandy space of ten square miles set nearly twenty feet above the river—surrounded by limestone hills ranging upward to several hundred feet.

Limestone caves of the hillside welcomed them for cool respite on hot summer days. They lounged in the wato prairie grass on the side of hills while watching deer feed in the late afternoon sun and shadows. They walked for miles across the ridges to gather berries and nuts in season and to visit tribal relatives in the outlying area. All of the time they enjoyed the wonder of Great Spirit Wakantanka's many glories.

WEE-NO-NAH WAS A RESPONSIBLE child who completed all tasks assigned. She was schooled in the ways of the Native Americans, understanding the shared ownership and the responsibility of providing for family and tribe. A trusted child with good sense who seldom needed correction, she did her part with ease and aplomb.

Following the traditional ways, she was trusted to do what was right—and succeeded. Wee-no-nah's mother encouraged her daughter in her days spent with Morning Star, knowing the background of the family, including her part in christening him "the Peaceful One."

Together Wee-no-nah and Morning Star worked on their schooling in the Dakota alphabet, as well as learning some few words of the white man. The Dakota alphabet often paralleled the sounds of the English language, but words were considerably different. They worked to create simple sentences:

Wee-no-nah said, "Zitkadan dowanpi." ("Birds sing.")

Morning Star offered, "Wa skaj." ("Snow melts.")

They moved on to form their own creative sentences. As Wee-no-nah enjoyed her singing, Morning Star offered, "Wee-no-nah olyokipiya dowan." ("Wee-no-nah sings beautifully.") As Morning Star enjoyed his hunting, she countered with, "Morning Star tahca cepa topa o." ("Morning Star shot four fat deer.")

They learned that within their Dakota language there were four dialects—the Santee, Yankton, Teton and Assiniboin. With assistance from parents and older children of the village, they soon became adept at moving from the Dakota language (also known as Lakota in the Teton dialect) to

Grosbeak, hand-rendered carving. *Author's collection.*

English. They were admired for their skills and encouraged by the villagers to continue their learning.

Elders at communal campfire in the evenings often told of the Great Sky and of their blood brothers of the West. Someday Morning Star and Wee-no-nah would visit Native American relatives of the Great Plains and the grand mountain ranges beyond.

Chief Wah-Pa-Sha was a great leader to his people. Over the years, he led warriors in battles ranging north to Canada. He was warrior, peacemaker and acknowledged leader of his tribe. He served as emissary to the English governor in Canada (Quebec) and to the government in Washington, D.C. On one occasion of ceremony in Canada, he was awarded a red cap in recognition of his efforts. From that point forward, he was known as "Red Cap."

The fighting had passed by the time Wee-no-nah and Morning Star were coming of age in their peace-filled surround, enjoying their times with Wah-Pa-Sha. They found special interest in stories of the stars, of linkage to ancestors and the Indian sign language he demonstrated. They used his sign language as they ventured into the woods to try to communicate without words.

The key signal for either was that of "friend"—two fingers upraised above the palm at shoulder height. They learned from Wah-Pa-Sha that there were more than seven hundred word signs used to communicate. Although they used symbols like "sunrise" and "listen" and "talk," they especially liked the symbols for "true" and "heart" and "good"—their usual expressions one to another.

Wah-Pa-Sha watched Wee-no-nah and Morning Star grow. Along with other parents and village elders, he watched over them and guided them as they matured into beautifully talented young tribal members. Arms and legs stretched to exquisite and perfect proportions. Each stood tall in the midst of their peers. They moved in their quiet days in the woods with the sleekness of deer observed and hunted.

Wee-no-nah was tawny, beaming and energetic. She spent many of her days with her mother learning the ways of the traditional household. She cooked meals over the open fire, planted and tended the small garden plot and watched over her younger brothers and sister—as expected of one moving to full maturity. The basic hunting, fishing and gathering tools she learned offered her great strength, capability, resilience and sustenance in aiding family and village diet.

Morning Star, with his father and other young men, used the bow and arrow throughout all seasons. With arrowheads sharpened and practiced aim developed since childhood, he took all manner of wild bird and beast. Although corn and squash and sunflowers were occasionally planted, crops were neither large nor consistent. Gathered wild plants and roots provided a balance for cooking. Hunting provided for year-round sustenance.

Fishing in the Great River and hunting in the valleys brought many wonderful feasts in days of good weather. Dried foods helped to carry tribe members through the scarcity and harshness of winter, when meals were often scant. For days on end there would be no food. A shared small bird roasted on the fire brought but a taste to a growing young body. A dried root cooked over the fire provided a broth to be shared by many. A part of the preparation of youth was to learn how to fast—since the reality of starvation was often near at hand.

IN SPRING AND EARLY winter, Morning Star trapped and fished the frigid backwaters of the Great River. Fishing in late autumn provided him with more than sufficient meals for his family. Along with fish large and small, the sloughs provided squirrel, muskrat, beaver, otter and mink in abundance. Netting the fish for smoking and the trapping of fur-bearing animals for pelts allowed him a strong inventory to trade.

To prepare his fish, Morning Star laid out the cleaned whole fish on a rack of fresh saplings. Making his pe'ta (fire), nimble fingers quickly worked a bow and spindle into a hand block to generate heat, smoke and spark. In seconds, the ember glowed—to be gently placed on dry tinder. As with his continuing dance with Wee-no-nah, his fire making was a dance, a romance.

In a small tipi constructed for his purposes, he kept the coals burning softly for several days as fish were properly aged and seasoned. On occasion, he created pemmican (a seasoned meat mixture) that was dried and smoked in a similar fashion. Due to reliance on meat as a main source of nourishment and sustenance, pemmican was a staple of the Native American diet. His production, expertise and sharing were enjoyed and appreciated by all the extended family members.

With Morning Star, Wee-no-nah often visited the missionary/trading post established by French explorers on the other side of the river for trading.

Rainbow and brook trout. *Author's collection.*

Pemmican, a "new" source of nourishment to visitors, had great appeal to those coming to the trading post. Pemmican was lightweight and traveled extremely well for Native Americans and frontiersmen alike. It served to further Morning Star's trading experiences and inventory.

The fish and furs and pemmican led him to treasures previously unseen. He was able to provide coffee for his family, candy treats for his younger siblings and a special blanket for his mother. For Wee-no-nah, his young love, he traded several of his finest furs for a book titled *Wasicun Ka Dakota Ieska Wowapi*, an English-Dakota dictionary. Since her early learning of the English and Dakota alphabets, she had become totally infatuated with the sounds and rhythm of words and loved seeing those words in print.

When visiting the mission, Wee-no-nah would always take time to seek out the resident priest and expand further her word experiences. She became adept at English and her native tongue (Iapi) with the help of her mother. Through conversations with the missionary, she added a few words of French.

She may also have extended her spiritual beliefs. All Native Americans are spiritists, believing that spirits of their ancestors take interest in their daily activities. With learning and association with the missionaries, Wee-no-nah and some of her friends came to believe that the French priests were actually messengers from God and thus revered them. They called them "good spirits."

In his trades at the mission, Morning Star chose for his revered Chief Wah-Pa-Sha a red wool scarf to wear with his red cap. He knew how much the chief valued the red cap given as an honor for his role in peacekeeping. Morning Star hoped that the scarf would offer similar recognition of the influence one so close had given to him throughout his young life.

For himself, he had his sights set on a new musket rifle. But that would take many more skins and far more fish. In another season of hunting, trapping and preparation of his special food products, he hoped to build a sufficient account with the trader to allow him to order the superb gun seen at the

Vintage bows. *Author's collection.*

post. Although a very skilled marksman with the bow and arrow, he knew that his prowess as a hunter would greatly increase with the rifle.

These were peaceful times, and there was no need for anyone to look on the possession of a masterful weapon by a Native American youth approaching his eighteenth birthday as any challenge to the peace. Chief Wah-Pa-Sha recognized that the times were changing for the best. There was no need for war. Battles had been fought for many years, and resulting consolations had been made in their lands and in their traditional lifestyle.

Morning Star and his friends could not venture and hunt in the same fashion or range that Wah-Pa-Sha had as a young hunter. Through Wah-Pa-Sha's recent visit to Washington, D.C., as representative of his people, he was brought to ever-greater awareness of the power and development of these visitors to his land. They had virtually taken over the entire country. Traveling by train to Washington, he understood the enormity of the country and the astonishing changes in the culture. It was a time for recognition and resolution.

THE LOVE BETWEEN WEE-NO-NAH and Morning Star continued to grow. They were continually together yet went their separate ways as hunter and maiden. Morning Star found his place among the young men. His peers respected him for his hunting, fishing and trapping skills. He was an accomplished lacrosse player and held his own in all of the contests of strength and bravery on the sand prairie.

Fellow youth and council elders recognized his skills as horseback rider and man of the river. He often led the young men on overnight forays into the woods, where he taught them skills of being men of the woods. Utilizing knowledge gained from his father, Waditaka, and his mentor, Chief Wah-Pa-Sha, he demonstrated necessary survival techniques in all of the seasons of the year.

He led hunting parties and guided youth of the village in the ways of the river. He demonstrated the nuances and intricacies of paddling the tanpawata across the small lake or into the backwaters of the Great River. He traversed the hills and crossed the partially frozen waters of late fall and early winter in pursuit of game and in the daily care of his traps.

Wee-no-nah's life since earliest days centered on Morning Star. He was there outside the tipi each morning to greet her and wish her a blessed day under the big sky. He made her laugh. With him she was openhearted in every way. He told her stories often that began with, "Once upon a time…."

Garvin Heights forest scene, Winona, Minnesota. *Author's collection.*

Hand-rendered model of Wee-no-nah and Morning Star. *Author's collection.*

They were stories that he had heard in the wigwam when the elders gathered. There were stories of the stars and the rain and the wind. There were stories of the great buffalo herds and hunts, of the healing powers of the medicine man and of Wakantanka, who watched over them from above. Morning Star made up stories as they sat in the meadow or by the side of the rushing creek. They were stories of escapades of Native American braves and warriors who had come before—stories of hunting and physical prowess and horsemanship.

From Wee-no-nah, he learned new words of English and blended them into his stories. He watched her as she sewed with her mother, as she became an able cook at the campfire and as she grew as a woman. He was able to balance time spent with her against time spent with his peers.

He was led by parents and traditions of the tribe to know that he was to be hardy and firm as hunter and leader. Yet the expectation was that his gentle side of living was to be treasured above all. In care of horses and all animals, in the treatment of the earth and in thankfulness for Wakantanka's many blessings, he was a natural leader. Each young man was taught to revere his elders and the achievements of ancestors. One was to show extreme care for his soul mate. It was not a suggestion. It was clearly an expectation that Morning Star would be true to his heart and to his love, Wee-no-nah.

WEE-NO-NAH CELEBRATED HER SIXTEENTH birthday with a feast prepared in her honor by her parents. She was given a beautiful deerskin dress made by her mother to recognize her passing into full adulthood. It had not been discussed, but she assumed that she would soon hear the words "Yu'ze kta yustanpi" (She is engaged)—the words that Wee-no-nah wished to hear more than any others.

The Indian rite of betrothal was completely at the determination of the father of the potential bride. All followed and understood the rules clearly. The father had the final say. Even though Wee-no-nah and Morning Star had spent a lifetime together and fully expected to marry, they knew that Wah-Pa-Sha was the decision-maker, the one to prevail.

They did not have an option. They could not "run away," since this was forbidden. They were members of the tribe and expected to live their total lives within the tribe, unless the chief allowed differently.

Unbeknownst to Wee-no-nah, her father had recently engaged in council with some traders who had visited the post and their village on the sand prairie. They were French explorers who were sent by their government in

Partial image of statue of Wee-no-nah. Windom Park, Winona, Minnesota. *Author's collection.*

Canada to visit other established French settlements at Trempealeau (known as the "Moved Mountain"), Wah-Pa-Sha's Prairie and LaCrosse.

The early Winnebago name for the Trempealeau locality of Hay-ne-aw-chaw was translated by Hennepin La Montaigne to be "qui Trompe-a L'eau"—or the Mountain that Was "Getting Pretty Wet." The Winnebago name of the locality, Wa-kon-ne-shau-ah-ga, meant "the Place of Rattlesnakes on the River."

Snakes were indeed prevalent in the countryside surrounding Wah-Pa-Sha's Prairie (also known as Ke-ox-ah). Sunning on the sides of the limestone cliffs several hundred feet high, rattlesnakes could be found from LaCrosse on the south all the way to Red Wing's territory on the north. With the landing of the most recent French boats at the village of Ke-ox-ah on the sand prairie, possibly some other snakes came ashore, for life would never be the same for Wee-no-nah or Morning Star.

As WEE-NO-NAH MOVED THROUGH the exciting months of her emerging young adult life, she became ever more in love with Morning Star. He was fast becoming the young leader of his small band of peers. Chief Wah-Pa-

Sha continued to recognize Morning Star's prowess and often selected him to lead hunting parties—a right generally ascribed to much older braves. The young braves easily followed him and often teased him that he would soon be appointed to the chief's elder council—a high honor reserved for the greatest of warriors.

Together Wee-no-nah and Morning Star made frequent trips across the river to the post and mission, to be warmly greeted. All acknowledged Wee-no-nah's skills and beauty. Learning the spoken French language from the missionaries, they invited her in turn to be a teacher to them of the ways and words of the natives.

Combined with the strengths and easy manner of Morning Star, the traders and missionaries viewed them as the ideal couple of Ke-ox-ah village—those with whom to grow future relations. From paddling Morning Star's tanpawata up and down the river, they were well known. They visited villages of La Crosse and Trempealeau on the south and the village of Wing's tribe to the north as emissaries of Chief Wah-Pa-Sha, staying with those whom he had designated.

They traded some of their treasures from the trading post for unique artifacts of fellow villagers. Morning Star accompanied young braves on hunting and fishing ventures to yield new friendships and a bounty of game for villagers. Wee-no-nah shared stories of the French, as well as her special talent for languages. Young maidens were mystified by her words and by the wisdom she had gained at such a young age.

The young couple learned of the ways of those who lived elsewhere on the Great River. Other tribe members always sent them off with blessings as they left each of the villages. Admired for their skills and their obvious love for each other, it was expected that this young couple would provide leadership for many years to the Native Americans of the Hahawakpa region.

Upon return from their travel to Wing's village one summer day, Chief Wah-Pa-Sha summoned Morning Star to council. Elders of the tribe were assembled in the tipiwakan meeting house at the edge of the Great River. Chief Wah-Pa-Sha pronounced to the council and to Morning Star that he had been in negotiations with the French traders over past weeks.

Announcing to elders and to Morning Star that having sought counsel from Oyannke oeoka, the true medium, and from spirit Woniya, his decision was now clear. Wee-no-nah was to marry the son of the leader of the French trading party. She would leave with the group for Quebec in their large tahukawata bullboat within the week. As father and chief, his decision was made and supported by the tribal council—it was final.

MORNING STAR VIEWED THE decision as unconscionable. He had formed such a great bond with Wee-no-nah and with Chief Wah-Pa-Sha that it was unbelievable to him that such a decision could be made. His entire life had revolved around growing in the family and in the tribe. Now he was to lose all. In his life with Chief Wah-Pa-Sha, he strove to represent the best of tribal commitment and devotion. He had given every remaining part of his heart to Wee-no-nah.

Upon hearing the news, Wee-no-nah was distraught. The pronouncement her father had made left her nowhere to turn. She counseled with her mother, pleaded with her father and shared her lament with Morning Star. The young couple discussed the possibility of running from their home village but knew that it was forbidden. They would be outcasts forever.

Wee-no-nah walked with Morning Star on the trails, rested with him on the hillside overlooking the village and promised to be his forever. In the late afternoon sun and shadows, their mood grew even more gentle and tender. Holding his hand in the prairie grass, she appealed with him to Wakantanka, their God of all, for mercy and forbearance.

Morning Star knew that they had no recourse—the chief had spoken. He promised Wee-no-nah that he would devote his life to her. He would seek permission to go from the village and live a life of solitude and devotion to her ideals. He would use his many skills and abilities to support himself.

By horseback and by tanpawata, he would traverse the lands and water and learn the woksape wisdom of the medicine men of the villages they had visited. He would become a guide to others—always with Wee-no-nah's goodness and love to support him. Upon arrival back in the village, he would seek the permission of Chief Wah-Pa-Sha to be set free.

Wee-no-nah promised to honor the memory of her true love for the rest of her life as well. Like Morning Star, she, too, had a plan. Knowing that she could not bear to live a moment with anyone other than Morning Star, she had decided to give her life to Wakantanka—by joining the blood of her ancestors in the Big River. She did not share her plan with Morning Star.

AFTER A TEAR-FILLED FINAL moment in the setting sunlight, the beautiful young maiden and the love of her life returned to Ke-ox-ah, as they knew they must. Wee-no-nah changed to her finest dress and accompanied Morning Star to council with her father.

After discussion with the chief and council, permission was granted for Morning Star to leave in just days to begin his new life venture. Much was said of the council's exceptional support for Morning Star, of his strengths and the wisdom he would bring to generations to follow. Morning Star, Chief Wah-Pa-Sha and the village elders smoked the peace pipe to signify harmony, peace and mutual trust. Little was said of the chief's decision about his firstborn daughter.

Upon parting, Morning Star tended to his horse and his belongings. Wee-no-nah crossed the sand beach and cast off from shore in her father's tanpawata. She set off across the river to follow the east shore of Hahawakpa northward as the sun was setting. Guiding herself first by the final colors of the day and then by familiar landmarks of bluffs and riverside at moonlight, she paddled with ease toward the sacred place of her ancestors, Wisdom Point.

Overlooking a large lake formed by the juncture of the Hahawakpa and Sapa (Black) Rivers, this imposing outcropping of limestone bluff was renowned as a place to settle the spirit and to come to a full decision. At the very peak of the bluff, she would light her Miniwakan petizanzan spirit lamp and seek the counsel of Wakantanka.

Wee-no-nah, daughter and firstborn child, was dressed in her finest—the hand-sewn tawny dress of deerskin created by her mother on the occasion of her sixteenth birthday. The beautifully stitched dress was adorned with beads of many colors. The quietly muted green and red beads had lost some of their sparkle and luster after two years of wear, but they perfectly suited the autumnal tones of foliage she had seen on this last day with her true love. The blue beads matched the sky overlooking the valley on the day of her birth.

She stood at the top of a three-hundred-foot limestone rock outcropping at the side of the Great River. Surrounded by the beautiful hills and valleys, she was at peace, albeit oiyokisica (mournful). This was her home, her land. For miles around her, she could see the silvery river shimmer in the moonlight.

The sap that flowed through the hardwood trees around her was as blood to her veins. The shining water moving in the river below contained the blood of her ancestors. Every part of the earth was sacred to her. Every sandy shore, every eagle overhead, every leaf of the tree was holy in her memory and experience. The river was her brother. She was at home.

With one final request to Wakantanka, her God of all, she set aside her moccasins and stepped off the ledge to a life with the ancestors of her Dakota Sioux tribe.

Full image of statue of Wee-no-nah. Windom Park, Winona, Minnesota. *Author's collection.*

Original vintage painting, artist unknown. *Author's collection.*

UPON LEARNING OF THE terrible loss of his soulmate, Morning Star gathered his belongings. Tipi, wooden traps, new spring-loaded traps and sets gained from the traders, blanket and drawings by Wee-no-nah were all covered with oiled skins of deer to rest on a travois (framework of poles) pulled behind his horse. The tanpawata and paddles rested at the top of a pallet, all tied down with leather thongs.

With a heart of stone, Morning Star set out to cross the river. Traveling north to Wing's village, he found the pole boat fashioned by villagers to traverse the river in a relatively flat and shallow place. Using ten-foot poles, the villagers guided Morning Star and his possessions across the river.

As he traveled the east side of the river south to Wisdom Point, Morning Star visited the site of Wee-no-nah's death plunge onto the rocks. He communed with Wakantanka, requesting ever-lasting life for his beloved.

Moving some miles downstream, he found a small island offshore to which he could walk the horse. He set up his tipi and created a sparkling fire on a full moon night at the water's edge. He would reside for the rest of his life on the Great River—in the shadow of the bluff from which Wee-no-nah perished.

A Double-Eagle Bike Ride

Let's take a bike ride down memory lane. One glorious summer afternoon, you can easily coast along beside me. I'll be the easy, nonpaid tour guide. We'll oil our chains and crank up single-speed bikes to explore a bit. Although my legs will pull harder on the bicycle than they did sixty years ago, my memory will have sharpened. My love for Winona and the Hiawatha Valley has never waned.

We'll start at Princess Wee-no-nah's statue and fountain at Windom Park in the heart of town. We might review her various placements in the city and the absence of the stone turtles with whom she formerly abided. We'll cruise our single-speed Schwinns west on Fifth Street to pass "the Hub," Swede's Bar, "the Rec," West End Theatre, Mahlke's Bakery and the West End Hotel. We'll view the Cozy Corner, Tubby's Oasis, Libera's Grocery and Roger's Meat Market—with its historic smell of smoke and garlic-laced Turner's Sausage. Maybe we can find an original 1870s brick or two peeking through the Fifth Street roadway.

Eating a fresh chunk of sausage from Roger's Meat Market, we can stand across the street in front of the West End Bait Shop and view the historic Schuler Chocolates building next door. Curving west on Fifth behind the Dairy Queen, we'll follow the route Barnum and Bailey Circus performers and animals walked on Circus Day of the 1950s, plodding out toward the airport.

Rising very early on a hot summer Circus Day morning, friends and I watched the sunrise unloading of animals and equipment from a special

Vintage bicycles and riders. *Courtesy Winona History Center.*

eighty-five-car circus train on Second Street. From the riverfront near Peerless Chain, we walked along with the animals through downtown to Fifth Street. Hopeful for a morning job of helping set up the massive tent with payment being a free circus ticket, we trekked all the way on Fifth from downtown to Forty-Fourth Avenue in Goodview, passing our home Grand Street and waving to neighbors. Our destination: the empty, sand-prairie acres of Goodview, home of circuses, baseball games and stockcar races on alternating days and evenings.

A little farther down the road on our ride, we rediscover the site of the Sky-Vu Drive-In, home of "Buck Night." Across from the "Happy Landing," an adult beer joint serving up pitchers of Bub's Beer, dancing and fun for decades, we would line up our jammed cars on most Tuesday evenings of 1950s summers. On old Highway 61, all were admitted for a "buck per car," where we awaited the wonders of outdoor viewing, teenage exploration and second-run movies through the two-part windshield of our '50s car. With one speaker hanging inside the left or right front window, we enjoyed monaural sound akin to that of the movie projector in "Bugsy" Moore's tenth-grade biology class.

On nearly every summer day except Circus Day, we could head on past the drive-ins to "the Pits." Today, pedaling past Airport Road and the former May's Root Beer Drive-In, we arrive at the Sand Pits on our left. Lucky ones of us spent days of high school summer in this place of mounded, quarried sand and deep, spring-fed artesian pools. The warm sand beach offered Winona a teenage version of *Beach Blanket Bingo*.

A wholly unsupervised place for teenagers, there was beauty, adventure and cool fun during hot days. Most of the time, my summer job at the Owl Motor kept me on task. But on weekends with my girl, or in the dark of night with "the boys," I occasionally walked across the well-known sliding sand piles.

A large sand and gravel lot fronted the property. Filled with large cement trucks, cement blocks and a tall sand tower, it was home to Matzke Concrete Company. At night, great shadows engulfed us as we quietly snuck across the huge parking lot in bright moonlight toward the accumulated dunes.

Unfortunately, our bike ride of today must detour, as we are faced with trailer park residences blocking entrance to the enchanted land. We turn our bikes around and double back a few blocks to take one of the sandy east–west streets across the ultra-flat sand prairie. Avoiding sand burrs reaching out to grab us, we soon arrive at today's "new" Highway 61 (new in the 1960s).

Turning north on the shoulder for a mile or so, we park our "too cool," single-speed bikes and walk into the same "Pits" from the other side of the water, through the new Goodview Park on Highway 61. Having brought our own nickel bottles of Coca-Cola and a towel in the bike basket, we take a brief swim and enjoy a delicious frosty bottle of Coke on our sun- and sand-filled towel.

The sight is enough to hold us for the afternoon, but conversation with a local reminds us that across the highway is a beautiful, bluffside ride up to a laconic farm or two. We will pass the Biesanz Quarry—home of famed Winona limestone used for architectural facing on projects far and wide.

If we continued on our path, we could turn up Goodview Road past Boller Lake to meet up with Highway 14 at St. Mary's College and the former home of Beck's Brewery. Crossing over that road, we could visit the beautiful Gilmore Valley, head up the hill to Wilson and connect back to Highway 43 to take us down toward Sugar Loaf and into the east end of Winona, through the most glorious scenery imaginable.

Instead, we decide to turn west and north, keeping our oiled, chain-guarded and dusty bikes moving up Highway 61 toward Minnesota City. Making a left turn on County 248, we crank heartily—straight up the challenging hill to Rollingstone! After a several-mile challenge, we view Grandpa Rudy's old farm, pass Bonnie Rae's Café and Grocery, the feed mill and Norm's Tavern and zip by the Catholic church to head out west on County Road 25. From there, we will twist across uphill county roads through gorgeous hardwood forests surrounding the old Luxembourg community.

We take a much-needed peanut butter sandwich break on one of the many scary overlooks and their narrow, crushed-rock road intersects. Traversing the glorious valleys, we pass through Lewiston to visit the nearby tranquil cemetery at the Silo corner, a resting place for the eldest brother who introduced me to these hills. Enticing us to turn farther west are the towns of Altura and Bethany.

Around the corner and up the hill to Bethany, we could easily find friends, fresh apple crisp and a pleasant country visit on the family farm of Oscar Ties, early settler of the area. From there, we could travel on to the Altura Creamery, where one could only hope to find fresh, homemade, hand-dipped and double-stacked ice cream cones of the '50s.

If we are satisfied instead with fresh water from an outdoor spigot, we could whiz down the hill from Altura to pass Crystal Springs Fishery as we head to Whitewater State Park and the several branches of the Whitewater River that converge in nearby Elba. The Crystal Springs site enticed tens of thousands of observers to Sunday motorcycle hill climbs in the 1930s, welcomed our elementary school classes of the 1940s to the state fish-rearing ponds and invited the singular trout fly-fisherman to open casting.

It's the place of the Elba Store, home of "waxies," water worms and morel mushrooms (in season), nightcrawlers and some secrets to trout fishing. Mauer's Bar, down the street, displays record trout pulled from the waters. We could join in the camaraderie of trout fishermen, have a beer, swap stories and just try to gain a secret. Ha!

After a climb up the Elba Fire Tower, we might pass the buried town of Beaver and sit on the sandy shore of the Whitewater River, where as Boy Scouts we camped and heated our cans of beans over the wood fire. We would pass the former golf course and parade grounds where Boy Scout troops assembled and marched on sunny Sunday mornings.

But instead of an Altura and Elba run, we stay on County 25 out of Lewiston to Township Road 12 and slide by the Century Farms of the Nahrgangs, Wirts and Millers—all customers of the milk route from which I hauled milk to the Pleasant Valley Creamery in Winona as a fifteen-year-old. I double-shifted my old Ford F-1 into creeper gear as I tracked away from

A SHARED ASIDE ON THE TRAIL

A special remembrance of this area included a wonderful fall afternoon spent many years ago with my Uncle Arnold and Aunt Beth at their small farm and home near Lewiston. Just east of town was the tranquil setting where Arnold worked the fields with his team of horses. Bess was one. Who can name the other? Babe?

Arriving for lunch, my new young wife and I were overwhelmed with the typical farm lunch of mashed potatoes, roast beef and gravy—followed by Beth's homemade apple pie. Her warm baked goods were a constant and special delight when brothers and I visited the farm as kids.

A more beautiful sight cannot be found than the fields and hardwood forest surrounding the old brick house with a working windmill, hand pump and a "greening" apple tree right out the front door. I wish for the opportunity to take just one more trip into those woods for squirrel hunting, as I did with my girl during high school days.

Arnold and Beth were wonderful hosts who made the afternoon fly and provided us with insights into family. Arnold's quiet style and Beth's effervescence will always be remembered, as will the smell and warmth of their farm kitchen.

They exemplify the best of folks in the valley.

Lewiston Hill and up the steep, crushed-rock, county road on snowy days to gain a load of eighty-pound cans of milk destined for glass milk bottles and marvelous ice cream.

BACK ON OUR BIKES, we follow Garvin Brook down the hill toward the tiny Arches settlement. From there, we ride to and under the arches of the railroad bridge fronting the nearby Farmers Community Park. We soak our toes in the cool trout stream running aside gorgeous limestone walls. The home of picnics, Lutheran church services, family touch-football games and general outdoor fun, the park has served generations.

WPA Historic Pavilion, Farmers Community Park, the Arches, Stockton, Minnesota. *Author's collection.*

There are memories of hundreds of hours spent here over the years—from school patrol picnics where we could eat all the hot dogs we wanted to Lutheran church open-air ceremonies on summer Sundays to family gatherings and Sunday afternoon autumn "sweetheart" rides.

Leaving the Arches for a few miles east on Highway 14 to Stockton, we pass the place near Jack Oevering's home farm, where the author inadvertently dumped his trusty pickup truck and three thousand pounds of milk on the highway after a collision and rollover. In moments, we come upon the recently flooded village of Stockton.

Our bike trek circles around the bluff to avoid the five-hundred-foot climb up Highway 14's Stockton Hill—instead taking County Road 23 through the flat alluvial valley of the hill's backside. We again skirt Minnesota City, the Oaks Supper Club and the famous highway sign of the bar on Highway 61 that offered, "Ham On Rye—We Stack It High!!!"—to end up back at Goodview.

By circling the hills, we missed the chance to visit Tiger Lily's Tattoos in the old Swede's Bar across from the church. If we had a big basket on our bike, we could have taken home a twenty-five-pound cloth bag of Stockton Roller Mill Flour. We have also missed the ride by the Novitiate at the top of Stockton Hill and the breathtaking view of Gilmore Valley and St. Mary's College as we come around the final downhill curve. To think of it is to take one's breath away!

Any time spent on or near the Mississippi River and in the Hiawatha Valley from Lake City to LaCrosse is time banked in heaven. When we return to this area of bluffs and Indian mounds and God's great gifts of natural wooded land and streams, we are in a Garden of Eden.

The apples of Dakota and LaCrescent and Galesville (Wisconsin) are the sustenance of life and the exemplification of beauty. Using a multi-speed bike and scheduling an overnight or two, we could take a tour from Winona to Rushford to Houston to LaCrescent to LaCrosse to Galesville to Trempealeau to Nelson (Wisconsin) and back to Wabasha and Winona.

You will have traveled the route of our great-grandparents. The total route was probably well beyond the scope of their travel, but it was the area traveled by my girl and me nearly every Sunday afternoon. As teenagers and young marrieds in our 1949 Ford coupe or 1952 Nash cruiser or 1955 Plymouth four-door, we were guaranteed one of the best days of fall (and life) we could ever hope to spend.

IT'S ONLY FITTING THAT we conclude our trek over the hills and valleys with a bottle of wine at lakeside in Winona. Small plastic glasses fit easily into our hands. Kickstands down, our mood of mutual accomplishment and natural enjoyment that carried us over the hills puts us at ease. Overlooking Sugar Loaf from Lake Park, we are full of pride—toasting the allowance of another day in "God's Country," our Hiawatha Valley.

Next time, "Come on along!"

Markin' on the Twine

A Day on the River

I was there on the Mississippi. We traveled around, and occasionally across, "wing dams" constructed by our grandfathers. We landed our boats on islands of dredged sand removed by the Army Corps of Engineers to uphold the river's "nine-foot channel." Sunbathing and waterskiing were our forte.

In the summer as teenagers, we practically lived on the river. Someone's dad's sixteen-foot lapstrake boat with a twenty-five-horsepower outboard engine took us into the backwaters and onto the islands for sunning and skiing or overnight campouts. There was some danger with towboats, barges and boat traffic filling the waterway and moving every which way. We occasionally skied behind the wake of the barges. On sunny weekends, boats were flying in every direction across the channel from Homer Island, with neighborliness on the islands a constant.

At night, the pace was more leisurely and focused. It was sort of a dangerous game of hopscotch as we headed up or downriver. We traveled from one lighted or reflective post to another in crisscross fashion from shore to shore. Following these shore-built reflective markers freed us from colliding with wing dams and manmade structures. A few miles downstream, Brother Bob recalled:

> *Buoys were anchored on the main channel end of the wing dams to act as "shoulders" like those of our two-lane highways. Red buoys were on the right side heading upstream and black ones on the other side. The black*

The *Herbert Hoover* tow and barge, heading upriver. Winona, Minnesota. *Courtesy Winona History Center.*

ones were called "can buoys" and red ones were "nun-shaped" — tapered to a dull point at the top. As long as the boats or towboat/barges stayed in between those buoys, they were good to go.

There were also channel markers. I don't know exactly how far apart they were, but I know there was one at the north end of Dresbach and the next one up was slightly north of Dakota. The channel markers had lights on them; the buoys did not.

As we wandered near the river or bridge at night in Winona, we could see the tow's massive searchlights sliding across the shore and reflecting into the sky. Bob could see those shining lights up close and personal from the front porch of the Dakota Store.

Meeting a barge on the river in a small boat at night got one's attention! In addition, major spring and summer storms caused floating logs and debris to be an often unseen and submerged hazard. Best advice is to stay off the river at night.

EARLY TRAVELS

In early days, it was a challenge for steamboat pilots to bring settlers to the Upper Mississippi. There was no nine-foot channel. On any upriver journey, sands beneath the rushing waters were constantly shifting. Someone had to hang out on the bow of the boat and constantly toss a heavy ball on a twine line into the water. From each toss, these early "gaugers" recovered the ball and called back a reading of fathoms (depth) of water to the captain.

"Mark Twain" was the shouted report from the seaman taking these soundings at the bow of the boat to indicate the depth of the water under the keel. In Mississippi riverboat dialect, "Mark Twain" was a shortening of the phrase "markin' on the twine," which was followed by the water depth in fathoms.

A fathom is equal to 6 feet or 1.8288 meters. It is a unit of length in the old imperial and U.S. customary systems, used especially for measuring the depth of water. There are 2 yards or 6 feet in an imperial fathom. Originally based on the distance between a man's outstretched arms, the size of a fathom has varied slightly. The name derives from the Old English word

Steamer *East St. Louis*, heading upriver, Mississippi River. *Courtesy Winona History Center.*

fæðm, corresponding to the old Frisian word *fadem*, meaning embracing arms or a pair of outstretched arms.

Samuel Clemens captured the essence of the gauger, taking up "marking on the twine" as his pen name Mark Twain—from that very action of measuring the depth of the water to prevent the paddle-wheeler from running aground. Clemens was licensed as a riverboat captain at age twenty-three in 1859, working two years at a monthly rate of $150 to $200. He is best known for *The Adventures of Tom Sawyer* and its sequel, *Adventures of Huckleberry Finn*.

ON THE RIVER

We marked our own way on the river. A turn at the bridge piling took us into Sam Gordy's Slough. We knew to avoid known wing dams as we circled into landing on one or the other of the islands. When pulling a skier, we stayed in the main channel. When we wanted championship-size sunfish, we searched new territory. We looked for ripples and a flat spot on the water—our usual, learned way of spotting the notorious (and beneficial) wing dams.

Brother Bob lived the life of the "river rat" at his home area of Dakota and Dresbach on the Mississippi. Our Uncle Frank had a tavern and boat rental on the specific spot of today's Lock and Dam 7. A few miles upriver, the Dakota Store faced directly onto the river. It was Bob's stopping-off place for .22 shells, cigarettes (twenty cents a pack) and candy bars. His home was just up the valley on eighty acres, where Grandpa had a small dairy farm from which he created his own milk route. He also raised strawberries, raspberries, hay and corn on the steep hillside.

Across from Dakota, before the navigation dams were built, the soon-to-be backwaters were farmland. Many of the sloughs are named after the farmer who had owned the land. The first few years after navigation dams were in place, the Army Corps of Engineers allowed townsfolk to go across the river on the ice in the middle of the winter with a team of horses and bobsled to harvest water-surrounded trees for wood to heat their homes. Bob recalled one incident when "Gene Peterson went across the river on the ice with a team and sled. On the way back, with the sled loaded, the team and sled broke through the ice—drowning team and driver."

Uncle Frank was the lucky one. He got to ride the trolley from water's edge up the three-hundred-foot limestone cliff to garner another load of

Fishermen on an original wing dam, 1930s, Mississippi River. *Courtesy Winona History Center.*

limestone chunks to be moved into the river to stabilize the meandering underwater sands near Dresbach and the new Lock and Dam 7. Grandpa Voigt had either owned or leased the property above the river to supply the necessary rock "riprap" in the 1930s to the Army Corps of Engineers.

As an adult, I sat anchored at mid-channel on one of Frank's "secret" wing dams, with both of us pulling in and filling our stringers with "lunkers." Conversing about early days on the farm at Dakota and finding out little things about my mother, Erika, who had died when we were all little kids, was a treasured moment on the Mississippi. Her elder brother Frank's words and the moments at mid-river were never to be duplicated.

Back at his small home in LaCrescent, Frank quickly filleted the "sunnies" for us to enjoy. Butter-fried sunfish fillets, cold Heileman's Old Style Beer from across-the-river LaCrosse (since 1858) and friendly conversation in a well-worn, comfortable kitchen was as good as it gets.

The Minnesota DNR warns us yet today of the danger of the "manmade rock piles" in its *Minnesota River Guide* (2015), showing the location of same. There are "hundreds to the north of the Minnesota-Iowa border"— virtually all underwater and unmarked. As kids, we knew where some were

Sleigh with team of horses and riders, January 2016. *Author's collection.*

in our favored areas of travel into sloughs and around islands, but we never had a map. Dangerous to cruise over a limestone rock pile and tear up the lower housing on one's motor. It was better to stay in the main channel. But fishing was always best back in the sloughs and over the wing dams. Uncle Frank and Bob knew their area, now the site of the new I-90 bridge over the Mississippi.

NEW CONSTRUCTION

In the 1930s, the U.S. Army Corps of Engineers constructed eleven locks and dams and associated "wing dams" for purposes of navigation ease and stability of the "nine-foot channel" north of the Minnesota-Iowa border. In the 1950s, we regularly ran these locks in a fifty-mile span from mile marker 753 at Alma, Wisconsin, downriver to mile marker 703 at La Crescent, Minnesota. We were in pleasure boats, fishing boats, duck boats and steel-hulled houseboats. Some of the guys even traveled from Winona to LaCrosse on the river in rubber tire innertubes.

When traveling on sunny days or star-filled nights, we meandered through the locks on our way from one place to another. Barges moved with us—often hogging the roadway (waterway) and the locks with their need to shuttle their many barges through in smaller multiples. We learned to stay clear of the towboats and their massive wakes—although we often skied over them.

The barge crews worked twenty-four hours, often on a six-on, six-off routine. They were well paid for their thirty-day constant assignment to the boat—and well fed. The Pletke Grocery of Winona cut out a particular niche of grocery service by supplying foodstuffs to the crews in their stops at Lock & Dam 5. A call by sea-to-shore radio to Pletke's as they came upriver created an order to be delivered to the lock. It was truly "front-door (shore) service" by grandson Paul, representing the well-acclaimed grocer's history since 1900.

Waters in the locks were raised or lowered depending on upriver or downriver direction. The DNR suggests that the constructed pools, locks and dams on the river are "steps in the river as it descends to the Gulf of Mexico." Dams created the pools and backwaters. To get upriver, one must be raised up to the next pool height. In the lock, a chamber opens on either end. If going upriver, water is added to raise the boats. Going downriver, water is released. There are truly "deceptive currents" and "dangerous turbulence" surrounding the lock and dam. The area 600 feet upstream and 150 feet downstream is a restricted area—with caution taken on entry or exit.

Lights (semaphores) guide us in and out as the massive gates open. There are mooring lines evenly spaced and hanging off the cement wall in the hundreds of feet of space. We must hold on to the line and *never tie it up* to the boat.

One of the most tragic accidents occurred when three high school juniors-to-be set out for a day on the river on August 26, 1959. As with the boys, these three young ladies borrowed a parent's boat and set off at 8:00 a.m. for a day of sand and sun on the Mississippi. The headlines of the afternoon *Daily News* reported a "Tragic Accident" and a "Fatal Dam Accident" that occurred when a sixteen-year-old young lady "Stabbed Herself in 5-A Lock."

The three young ladies were all class leaders of sports, the honor roll, the student council, GAA, the choir, English and Drama Club. Unfortunately, they didn't follow procedure of docking through the lock. They tied the boat to a lower rung of the steps in the sidewall. As the water came in to raise the level, the line became taut. The force of the water pulled the front of the boat downward toward sinking.

The boat's driver cut the line with a knife, with the resulting cut and snap of the highly stressed line forcing the boat to release and the knife to travel upward into her mouth and neck, cutting the carotid artery. The coroner offered that she probably didn't live but a minute or two.

Winter's icy backwaters also made for some great fun. With other Winona Boat Club members and their families at a Sunday afternoon winter fishing contest, we predrilled one hundred holes and lined up on the backwater ice with pole in hand to see who could win the prize. We truly enjoyed a sunny outdoor Sunday in January with others who cruised the river from May to November. Bottles of Bub's (Winona's first and best beer made in the caverns of Sugar Loaf) and LaCrosse's Old Style always added to the party flavor as we renewed acquaintances and caught "a slab or two." What a grand way to live.

The boathouse scene was alluring. On spring Saturday workdays, volunteers replaced old barrels with new to float the boathouses. Summer steak frys happened on the dock as evening came. A bonfire blazed. In a mélange of floating boathouses, houseboats and floral walkways, we celebrated the seasons. We even had a late summer luau—with authentic foods, colored lights, flowers and costumes. It was a festive time.

There were many summer and early autumn family boat trips up to Wally's Restaurant at Fountain City for dinner, where we enjoyed the finest of cuisine and company. We especially enjoyed the moonlit cruises. The ubiquitous Bub's or Hamm's or Old Style beer bottles (and twelve-ounce Pepsi bottles with ribbon-embossed logo) joined our journeys.

One especially luxurious weekend of boating with two boatloads of adults and family saw us traveling nearly one hundred miles from home. We spent three full days on the Mississippi. The first evening was spent at the old Lake City Hotel and the ballroom on the edge of town, with our second evening at the grand Lowell Inn of Stillwater.

Reservations had been carefully made of course. ("A party of twelve, please—in the Matterhorn Room.") We "dressed for dinner," as was expected at "the Mount Vernon of the West," with "in-laws" Fred and Eloise hosting our family party of eight. Fred enjoyed his accomplishment and his special after-dinner moment—a big cigar from the inn's glass case and his served "B and B" (Benedictine and Brandy) floated "just so," as Rusty so frequently did for Fred at Wally's. We floated home to Winona on a leisurely, sunny Sunday, with a dip in Lake Pepin along the way.

Lake Pepin Beach shoreline, Lake City, Minnesota. *Author's collection.*

Some years later, our family of six returned to the Mississippi for a day trip through bluff country. From Winona to LaCrosse we cruised the river, visited an island for a swim and bonfire hot dog lunch. Enjoying the sunshine and the beauty of it all, we arrived at midafternoon for overnight dockage and family fun at the LaCrosse Holiday Inn on the river. Our sixteen-foot orange Yarcraft stood the cruise very well, save for a near swamping by several huge river cruisers as they raced out of the lock at Dresbach. Cruiser drivers had little regard for small boats below, with waves nearly engulfing us.

Our adult daughter wondered, "How does one water ski on a mighty river with its scary currents?" She further suggested, "I often feel the pull of the river when thinking of Winona. An island party sounds mystical. The very personal and historic story of Uncle Bob's about the Armistice Day blizzard and the loss of his leg is fascinating. As someone not too familiar with the great river and its ways, it is quite a mystery with the lock and dams, wing dams, barges and log-sized catfish, not to mention the story Grandpa told of having to cut his boat away from a sinking boat in a slough or go down as well."

She offered the story from Grandpa Fred from memory: It was late afternoon. The small crew hadn't had much luck fishing in the backwaters of the great Mississippi. Storm clouds threatened. In the distance over the bluffs gathered a mountainous, dark-gray force, with veins of lightning threading through. Grandpa Fred knew, as the wind picked up, that they didn't have much time to get back to their boathouse and waiting T-bone steaks.

Eloise, Fred's wonderful wife of many years, and the Semlings—good friends, neighbors and fellow boaters of the moment—were also growing concerned. The murky brown water was getting choppy as they set off homeward at steady speed. Fred knew the sloughs well from years of exploration and fishing, being cautious as he made his way south. Glancing into one of the out-of-the-way channels near Prairie Island, he noticed some movement in the water. Swerving from the main channel to get a better look, he spotted a large skiff that had seen better days, and it was taking on water.

Fred made an easy decision to offer assistance. It was the way of the river. The boat's terrified occupants, a young couple and a six- or seven-year-old son, were soon pulled into the larger boat, using the ski ladder on the back. It didn't take much convincing to get the small family to abandon their rickety craft as Fred assured them that everything would be fine.

Family fun on a Mississippi River sand island, Homer, Minnesota, 1960s. *Author's collection.*

Underneath one of the seats was a thick rope for such emergencies. With the wind starting to blow, Fred attached the rope to the skiff and to a metal-chromed bracket on the back of *Jeffe*, his immaculate, nineteen-foot wood and mahogany Trojan Day Cruiser. With twin thirty-five-horsepower Johnson motors, the sturdy V-hull had plenty of power to tow the smaller boat back to the boathouse. It often pulled two water skiers up and out of the water at the same time.

Much relieved, the young visitors began to tell their tale. Fred and friend Al began the task of directing and slowly towing the sinking craft. As they began to move, the smaller boat took on even more water. With the additional weight and pressure, both boats were soon in danger of going down. The water's chop was growing from the storm. With strong waves, it wouldn't be long before all would be in danger and needing to swim for their lives. Fred realized that he had to act fast to avert disaster.

The young family was already quite shaken. They were on the verge of panic. The little boy was so afraid he thought it best to jump ship. Eloise thought fast to grab him as he was about to go overboard. All moved to the front of the boat as Fred scrambled to find his filet knife in the tackle box kept in the lower front cabin.

Jeffe, nineteen-foot Trojan Day Cruiser, Mississippi River, 1960s. *Author's collection.*

Moving to the taut rope, his hands shook as he pressed the sharp knife downward to saw at the thick rope. Not the best tool for the job, but it would have to do. Growing darker by the minute, with murky cold water surrounding his ankles, Fred worked quickly. Using all of his strength, which was considerable since he made a living lifting and hauling heavy vending machines, he made progress slowly.

As Eloise was pulling life jackets from under the seat, there was a loud *pop*. The boat lurched and tossed everyone forward into the open, small, mahogany-trimmed captain's cabin and wheelhouse. After a moment, they collected themselves, realizing that they had avoided disaster. The skiff was on its way to the bottom. With life jackets for all, they set off once again toward the boathouse.

Rounding the bend into the main channel, it began to rain, slowly at first and then driving like needles. The boathouse was soon in sight. With a turn of the captain's steering wheel, they were soon under the "old high wagon bridge" and into safe harbor.

Inside, wet, cold and shaken, all now had a story to tell their grandchildren.

TO CATCH A FISH

The thrill of an autumn day on the river with flights of mallards over open water, the spin of a dozen eagles coming off the rocks of adjacent three-hundred-foot limestone bluffs at Camp Lacupolis of Lake Pepin or of life itself is transforming. The symbol of our vast country is alive before me, majestically diving and swirling at the juncture of the Black and Mississippi Rivers as I stand on a mid-river sand island. It is easy to be enthralled.

We will leave our sand island campsite to start our day with a small-town breakfast at the old Alma (Wisconsin) Hotel on Highway 35 at 6:00 a.m. After meeting the locals and sharing the warmth of their hospitality and Alma's fine food, we can walk over to the river, hardly more than a block away. And we'll go fishing!

Putting up the signal flag at the boat landing at Alma behind the shops and old storefronts of another era, our early morning arrival gains us a ride across the channel from shore to a floating raft/snack shop/bait shop. We will spend the day fishing on the river at pools four and five, directly below the lock and dam. With food and fish cleaning services available (6:00 a.m.

Lock and Dam 5, Mississippi River, Winona, Minnesota. *Courtesy Winona History Center.*

to 6:00 p.m.) we will have unheralded outdoor entertainment for eighteen dollars. Pole rental and bait are available.

One needs a license. Not written, but acknowledged, is that cellphones are best left on shore. This is a day with God and his elements, a day of memory-making. Sheepshead, carp, massive catfish, paddlefish, northern pike, sauger, sunfish and crappies await—some of the 140 species and 25 sport fish present on the Upper Mississippi. One recent Great Alma Fishing Float outing with brother George was our last shared moment on the river—one when he caught white bass with impunity.

There are slow days and days of "line-busters," but opportunity exists every day for a boat ride from the dock behind the old riverfront at Alma to the fishing float. The abundance and variety of fish are overwhelming. The company is charming. When we're ready, we can grab the next shuttle to shore.

At the National Eagle Center of Wabasha, Minnesota, on the river, live eagles are within an arm's reach. Telescoping stands set up for our use by volunteers at riverside bring one's camera into eagle nests and into their singular flight patterns. There is majesty of bird and river.

The *Grumpy Old Men* movie of 1993 was filmed at Wabasha, starring Ann Margaret, Walter Matthau, Jack Lemmon and Burgess Meredith.

Stringer of sunfish, Wabasha, Minnesota, 2015. *Author's collection.*

Eagle at Wabasha, Minnesota. Author's telephoto image, 2013. *Author's collection.*

The follow-up, *Grumpier Old Men* (1995), brought Sophia Loren to town—and again included ultra-wise and occasionally obnoxious Burgess Meredith. The filmed catfish quests took us right into the backwaters of the Mississippi—and to the church wedding at Wabasha. We can visit the real Slippery's restaurant for a cold beer and a fish dinner, served with a bit of local flavor.

There is nothing better than a stringer of sizeable, sparkling sunfish or crappies caught on a sandy shore under an old bridge or off a wing dam on the Mississippi. Whether at Winona, Kellogg, Minnieska, Homer, Wabasha or Lake City, there are fishing holes to explore. If we choose, we can turn inward for a few miles to gain a midstream stance in the chilly, fast-flowing Whitewater or Root River or any of the hundreds of trout streams from Red Wing to Harmony—all to chase the ever-elusive trout.

With a little more searching of the small villages along the river, we can find delectable smoked carp. It is bound to be available from a local smoker. We just need to keep on asking and turning corners, eventually to meet a real "river rat" who knows his way around the river and the smokehouse. Wrapped in old-fashioned butcher paper, the golden fillets are huge—an invitation to an open-air picnic on a table overlooking the river.

With hometown Pepin Pickles, smoked carp, next-door Nelson Cheese factory cheese, bakery rolls from Stockholm and a bottle or two of local beer, we have the complete makings for an outdoor river valley meal, best enjoyed at the Maiden Rock overview of Lake Pepin. If only we had time for another local delicacy—coon and beans.

The river constantly invites.

Crossing the Monkey Bars

SEEKING PURCHASE AT HILLSIDE

In the woods too, a man casts off his years, as the snake his slough, and at what period soever of life, is always a child. In the woods, is perpetual youth….He who is not everyday conquering some fear has not learned the secret of life.
—Ralph Waldo Emerson, Nature, *1836*

We were on our way to the woods. The sun was shining brightly with promising blue sky and sunshine all the late July day. It was another day for hiking over and around the bluffs of our beloved Hiawatha Valley. It was a day to carry a canteen on a belt holder and a rucksack grab bag of essentials on one's back, tied with a rope across the chest. I needed both of my hands free for grabbing and climbing in the high hills.

Davey was similarly equipped, since we had together gained our outdoor essentials at the U.S. Army/Navy Surplus Store on Second Street. Mr. Roberts, the owner/manager, let us buy all manner of World War II military items returned (often unused) from across the seas. In our cellar stash we had a machete and hand grenade (welded shut), knives and rope, helmets, hatchet, tent and carriers, record and plot books and self-assigned military decorations of rank—along with *G.I. Joe* and *Sad Sack* comic books. Mr. Roberts's daughter, Shari, was a special friend who made our hearts do flips in fourth and fifth grades and on the playground.

Davey and I shared the same German-Lutheran Wisconsin Synod church, school, neighborhood, classrooms and teachers. With added after-school forays into his underground cellar, entered only through the outdoor folding "trapdoor" leading down a short staircase, or into the old shed of my backyard, we were forever together.

His house was easier to get to after school since it was right across the street from the school playground and kitty-corner from Deilke's Grocery Store, where we often hung out for a Pepsi or Popsicle. His Ma was always at home after school to greet us and offer a peanut butter sandwich or a cookie. She was a strong woman with an even stronger smile of welcome that put son and visitor at ease.

We were talking about Shari again as we started across the lake. We stopped at the lake bridge opening between the east and west parts of Lake Winona to take a look at happenings, of which there were usually none—unless some "lucky duck" hauled in a northern pike. It was the place where we usually fished. Best to be there, or at the end of Dacota Street under the big cottonwoods, early in the morning or near sundown, when mosquitoes usually kept us company.

Today was going to be a hot one. Our first stop was at the hand pump across the lake at the base of the hill known as Garvin Heights. In Bluffside Park, we filled our canteens with the cool water hand-pumped from the underground depths of limestone. Our intended trek for the

Lake Bridge and neighborhood, Winona, Minnesota, 2018. *Author's collection.*

day was to follow the old trail of crumbling cement steps from the park to the top of the hill.

The winding, narrow, two-lane road could be followed, but the straight-up path that someone had created fifty or more years ago was the less traveled path. It was seldom used and a real, unmet challenge—even for strong ten-year-old muscles. Our goal today was to get to the top, take a look at the city from our four-hundred-foot perch and then explore the backside of the hill. We would be fortified by a few of Davey's Ma's cookies, a can of Vienna Sausages and a few Schumacher's wieners each, to be roasted over a small fire built upon achieving the crest of the hill.

The first steps up the hillside were relatively easy. The lower third of the steps was a shortcut up to the road. Thanks to frequent use, it was relatively free of brambles. Having reached about one-third of the height of the hill, we crossed the hill road to continue our path upward. By the time we entered the enmeshed sumac and brambles of the upper side, we were in for a significant challenge. Weeds had overgrown, steps had become more deteriorated and covered with fallen limestone scraps and our climb seemed steeper—and a bit treacherous.

We were virtually standing straight up, while simultaneously getting a grasp and bending our scrawny legs around growth to push-pull our way upward. We hadn't made thirty yards upward beyond the road when we virtually ran out of breathing room, steps and handholds.

An open-furnace, high noontime heat coming off the limestone facing had replaced the cool summer breeze of lakeside. Washouts and limestone leavings left us with few solid step stones. How anyone could have built this original trail and steps was inconceivable. Striding upward was soon replaced by hand-over-hand pulls up the slope not unlike crossing under the monkey bars of the school playground. The only difference was that we were now hanging on—a few hundred feet in the air. Davey took one slide downward about ten feet or so, resulting in a strong scrape across his nose.

Using twisted limbs and unsteady footholds, we managed to take a break on the top of a large rock outcropping. As we sat, I reminded Davey of the pictures of workers we had recently seen crossing the faces of Mount Rushmore. In a display on the second floor of the Winona Public Library, sculptors appeared to easily move—vertically and horizontally—in chorus with a tangle of ropes and block and tackle attached from above. No doubt they had some steel-toed boots. Our U.S. Ked "tennies" just weren't doing the job. We needed those heavy boots and a personal, hundred-foot rope attached to our belts that was pinioned on the upper shelf of the hill. Where was our "go-to" plan?

We were reaching a point of no return. Previous experiences in the woods had us sliding on our backsides as we tumbled and slid down and through the snow. We had slipped on the trail of vegetation, leaves and mushrooms on a dewy morning in autumn woods and slid downhill for a ways to stain our corduroys in the tall grass. But we were relatively unhurt. This was a "different kettle of fish" into which we had ventured. We could not gain purchase by going upward—and our climb/slide down was nearly vertical. We were truly between a rock and a hard place.

Ralph Waldo Emerson (one of our favorites) said that fear needed to be faced. Author Judy Blume more recently observed what we already knew at age ten: "Each of us must confront our own fears, must come face to face with them. How we handle our fears will determine where we go with the rest of our lives—to experience adventure or to be limited by the fear of it."

We knew it intuitively. This was to be a learning experience that was not in the books and teachings of our third-grade teacher, Grace McLeod. She kept our nose to the grindstone in arithmetic and cursive writing but did little to spark the interests of ten-year-old adventurers. She certainly wasn't about ropes and Keds and high places. We were on our own.

As we sat, we established a target. About fifty yards to our right from our rock seat, we could see a draw with small trees seemingly growing out the sides of the hill and leading downward to the road. We needed to do a sideways venture. As we approached the draw, we could take the ropes from our back kits, toss the kits downward for later recovery and tie the ropes together to give us flexibility and support as we moved downward.

It would be a shared mission of joined hands and tossed ropes. Coaching and apprising each other, we drifted sideways to reach toward our target cut of the limestone facing. The shared rope length was good and sufficient as we tossed it over a branch at a time and lowered away. Once gaining a foothold, the rope was tossed to the other. And so we worked for what seemed an eternity, steadily teaming and encouraging and knowing our downward path. The greatest joy was to drop the final eight feet or so—to land in the soft limestone ditch at roadside.

As we munched on hot dogs made over the fire pit of Bluffside Park, we were pleased with our effort. Even though we didn't reach the pinnacle, we had learned a lesson of value. Crunching Ma's cookies, we were affirmed again by our friend Emerson when he offered, "When a resolute young fellow steps up to the great bully, the world, and takes him boldly by the

Garvin Heights Bluffside, Winona, Minnesota, 2018. *Author's collection.*

beard, he is often surprised to find it comes off in his hand, and that it was only tied on to scare away the timid adventurers."

The author wanders yet the hillsides and woods of his youth. He likes Emerson and sometimes thinks of singer Bette Midler's song "The Rose" as he pushes and pulls through life: "It's the heart afraid of dying that never learns to dance/ It's the dream afraid of waking that never takes the chance/ It's the one who won't be taken who cannot seem to give/ And the soul afraid of dying that never learns to live."

Gandy Dancers, Life Lessons and Intersections

A Railroad Story of Winona

The position of Winona on the River is one of great importance, and when her Transit Road is pushed out to the bend of the St. Peter's, and the North and South Roads connect, must make her at many seasons of the year, almost the head of navigation.
—Winona Argus, *first issue, September 1854*

W inona was the epicenter. With immigrants arriving, a need for lumber to build the West and bounteous wheat harvests needing to be moved to mills, railroads were soon rolling, evolving and connecting.

Commencing in 1854—only a few years after Winona's settlement in the shadow of Sugar Loaf—a charter was granted to prominent Winonans to create the Winona and St. Peter Railway. That railroad brought its first carload of wheat from Stockton to Winona in 1862. Officially opening in the spring of 1863, success was seen as imminent. A *Winona Republican* issue of 1864 said of the railroad, "Even now, in the infancy of enterprise, the gigantic proportions which it is yet to assume are foreshadowed. The stripling is already called upon to do the work of a giant. It will be the part of wisdom to confer upon him, as occasion demands it, the strength of a giant."

By 1864, they were hauling at capacity of their rolling stock. More than thirty miles of rail bed had been completed, soon reaching Rochester. By 1868, they were at Waseca. The year 1871 saw them completing the 165 miles to New Ulm to continue on to the Black Hills of South Dakota. The

CNW train engines 2326 and 2451 between Stockton and Lewiston, Minnesota. Farm Bureau Park, "The Arches." *Courtesy Winona History Center.*

year 1879 saw them as a strong force in Rochester, Mankato, Zumbrota, Chatfield, Plainview, Redwood Falls, Tracy and Gary on the Minnesota border—with gross income of nearly $1 million in freight and passenger revenue. "Long trains of lumber left this city for the west" for years thereafter.

Strong revenue also came from the land grant properties associated with the owned track lines. More than 150,000 acres of land were offered for sale by the railroad in 1865 in Winona and ten other counties, including advertised "Wheat Land" of southwestern Minnesota.

The Winona and St. Peter lasted until 1900, when it was subsumed by the Chicago and Northwestern Railroad. Early incorporators of the Winona and Southwestern Railroad heading south to LaCrescent were historic figures of Winona. R.D. Cone, A.B. Youmans, Henry Lamberton and William Windom, among others, were lumber barons and early designers of the city. Windom went on to greater designs as Minnesota senator and secretary of the treasury of the United States. When the sparks were settled and their line was built in 1872, the president of the corporation had become local resident William Mitchell, of Minnesota law school fame.

While I was walking home in the northwest wind-driven late afternoon of the 1950s, the sun was setting on another harsh day. It was a good day for bluebills in our beautiful river valley. I had ventured from school to Wayne's house for a few comic book moments. In late October, we sometimes

Original railroad bridge from Wisconsin to Winona, Minnesota, Mississippi River. Note the steamer in river. *Courtesy Winona History Center.*

enjoyed an outdoor basketball shootout on the playground, but the puddles had frozen and the wind was whistling. Better to head indoors for stove heat and hot chocolate.

The barracks-like room Wayne shared with three brothers had been built in the fashion of a summer kitchen as add-on to the small house. One brother, Donnie, recalled the exposed ceiling rafters. He said it was like having his own "jungle gym" set from which to stretch and pull. I remember the great warmth and the pungency of kerosene as we stretched out on the line of single World War II U.S. Army surplus bunk beds.

After an hour or so of planning, palaver and organizing in the kerosene stove–fired bedroom, I headed home in the dark of 5:00 p.m. On the way, I stopped in the small outdoor barn/shed where Donald, Wayne's father, had dumped a gunnysack full of flyers waiting to be cleaned. What a beautiful sight at this great hunter's feet. Gathered by Donald in God's surround of the Minnesota City boat harbor, it was a bounty to behold and a great dinner for the family of seven.

Donald was an early morning milk hauler from area farms to dairy. Even though he put in a full day of lifting cans and hauling by noon, he still found the time and energy for afternoon duck hunting, especially on a blustery day when the north wind chased the northern mallards and bluebills down from Canada. Wayne and brothers joined with their Pa for an afternoon or weekend hunt, as schedules and space in the small boat allowed. A pull of the outboard motor cord and Donald was headed into the channel and off to his favored point to space out a few dozen decoys. When not at work, the decoys rested in the dark of the truck box on top of freshly washed ten-gallon milk cans.

After brief words and an ever-present smile from Donald, I headed for supper on Grand Street. Leaving Wayne's dad and his passel of ducks, I was intercepted by a Milwaukee Road passenger train with lighted dining cars and real people—passing by but feet away from my stance on the sidewalk. Directly across from Wayne's place lay these tracks of the Milwaukee Road, bisecting the city in a north–south fashion. With the Chicago and Northwestern Station on the river at Huff Street and the Burlington Way Station in the slough across the river, we had trains running day and night through city and neighborhoods and up and down the river to St. Paul, Chicago and places west.

The morning "Hiawatha" of the Milwaukee Road RR, 1964, Peawaukee, Wisconsin. *Courtesy Winona History Center.*

"Hiawatha" train at station, 1964. *Courtesy Wikimedia Commons.*

As I waited for the train to pass my uphill space on the sidewalk, I observed the fine folks a few feet away readying for dinner and lounging in the beautiful, well-lit club cars. They looked like the fancy folks from California I had seen pictured in the *Saturday Evening Post*. Having had a classroom field trip on the same train to LaCrosse and return, I had a real feel for the ornate furnishings and the comfortable seats—rivaling the comfort of a 1951 Buick Roadmaster back seat in which I once sat.

These Milwaukee Road tracks were less than two blocks from our front door, as contrasted to Wayne's one hundred feet or so. All who grew up in the neighborhood did so with a learned fear of the tracks. Open intersections of street and track and the merging of tracks at crossover points meant potential death. There was no fallback. A stuck foot between rail and stone was nothing to be messed with. If we walked the tracks (which we often did), we jumped from tie to tie since tie spacing was irregular to our foot beat and stride.

Speeding trains crisscrossed our city of one hundred intersections without warning lights or drop-down barriers. Common sense for pedestrian or driver was the only real rule. Our reality was the "City Traffic Box Score" shown at the bottom of every crash story in the *Republican-Herald*—a ghoulish statistic.

THE GANDY DANCERS

In early days, track needed to be laid. Manpower was the answer. Once laid, with spring floods and ill-defined levees, the cities, small towns and railroad tracks along the river were continuous victims of massive floods. Crews were employed locally, urgently and often from a transient population to work the rails. Brother Bob, living on the farm, remembered that our Grandpa Frank (Franz) Voigt came off the farm daily for a few years in the late 1930s to be employed in the Dakota (Minnesota) section of the railroads. He was a "gandy dancer," apparently a skilled worker who drove the pins in to hold the rails in place.

"Gandy dancer" is a slang term used for an early railroad worker, the British equivalent of the term being "navvy" (from "navigator," the original builders of canals or "inland navigations"), for builders of railway lines, and "platelayer," for workers employed to inspect and maintain the track. In the U.S. Southwest and Mexico, Mexican and Mexican-American track workers were colloquially "traqueros." Before work was done by machine, the gandy dancer and laborers laid and maintained railroad tracks.

In my review, the term has been described as specific to those workers who built the track, although one text states that "layers of railroad track are hardly ever called gandy dancers," asserting that the job of the gandy dancer refers to "track examiners," ascribing their responsibilities as "checking ties, bolts, track, and roadbed for necessary repairs." However, most sources refer to gandy dancers as the men who did the difficult physical work of track maintenance under the direction of an overseer.

There are various theories about the derivation of the term, but most refer to the "dancing" movements of the workers using a specially manufactured 5-foot (1.52m) "lining" bar (which may have come to be called a "gandy") as a lever to keep the tracks in alignment.

The term has an uncertain origin. A majority of early railway workers were Irish, so an Irish or Gaelic derivation for the English term seems possible. Some have suggested that the name was coined to describe the movements of the workers themselves (i.e., the constant "dancing" motion of the track workers as they lunged against their tools in unison to nudge the rails, often timed by a chant; as they carried rails; or, speculatively, as they waddled like ganders while running on the railroad ties).

A May 1938 article in the *Republican-Herald*, featured as part of the Winona Newspaper Project at Winona State University, describes a scene repeated up and down the river by Franz and his associates:

> *There are citizens who think a circus is "The Greatest Show on Earth." This is because they've never seen a couple hundred soaking wet men, the big bosses and the gandy dancers, doing a piece of old fashioned railroading.*

And this kind of show has been going on a few miles above Hastings at the Mississippi River's edge since it was discovered early Wednesday that flood waters, imprisoned in a great natural pocket, had burst its rocky seams and, rushing out, pushed tons of soggy earth into the river leaving 150 feet of St. Paul railroad track swinging in the air as if it were a Chinese foot bridge. The tracks of the Burlington were washed into the river.

To repair the damage, work was begun at once to put a foundation under the hanging rails and to rebuild the washed away track. Officials expected to work most of the night to finish the job.

The drama, and it has many of the aspects of setting up a circus, is going on in a wild setting. On one side, with a camp train of ten cars at its feet, is a rocky bluff; on the other the swollen Mississippi. On the ground, and it is a mucky, swollen mess between these boundaries. The work went on all day Thursday and through the night as leaders assumed the responsibility for putting the railroad back together again.

Grandpa brought home several pieces of railroad track that he cut with a cold chisel. After marking the rail with hammer and chisel all the way around the track piece, he then repeatedly struck with a maul to break off the piece. According to Bob, these twelve- to fourteen-inch pieces were used on the farm as individual, portable tie stakes for a horse or cow. The animal could pull the piece on a rope to the fresh grass but could not pull it too far to escape. This writer has one of those pieces in his garage today, used at home on Grand Street some sixty years ago for hammered splitting of walnuts and hickory nuts and for assorted tasks like nail straightening. It is still in use today.

Only a few miles upriver from Dakota at the Winona Landing, in "a lonely section of Burlington track a mile south of Winona Junction," a section crew like Franz's worked hard to restore river damage below Winona in June 1943. The newspaper headline reported, "Section Hand Dies in Bunkcar Fight." After a full week in camp and on the rails, a fifty-two-year-old worker from Butte, Montana, arrived home to the bunk car drunk and disorderly at midnight Friday. With all the crew asleep, he was told to "shut up or leave."

Belligerent, he attacked and was struck by fifty-six-year-old William Jackson, "an old-timer in such crews" with an iron bar. He said, "I grabbed the iron bar in my two hands and swung in the dark at his head." Jackson was charged at Alma, Wisconsin.

The *Republican-Herald* reported, "It is the story of a grim battle in the dark, a dramatic chapter from the lives of three homeless men who toil day after day to maintain the roadbeds of transcontinental railroads—the gandy dancers."

A July 1917 accounting was made of camp dining rooms not unlike those of the railroad. "Every day in one hundred boarding camps, men who labor hard in the open are fed at a cost of eighteen cents a day. That is the maximum. To exceed that limit is to have the cook lose his job." The daily menu included, for breakfast, oatmeal, pancakes and smoked pig jowl; for dinner, boiled beef, boiled potatoes, red rice, bread, beets and pudding; and for supper, hash, rice, macaroni, bread with oleo, tea, peaches and hobo cake.

The tracklayers continue through today, with college-age youth finding long hours, hard work and good pay for their labors. Machines do the heavy lifting, but the torque of human bodies and independent muscle is essential. It is for each to become intimate once again with the frequently walked rail beds of youth.

WE WERE OFTEN "FIRST responders" to auto and train crashes of the neighborhood. We heard the crash, jumped on a bike and were there before police, newspaper photographer "One-Shot Kelley" or the tow truck operator from MerKohn, Borzykowski or Owl Motor. Open intersections and the "Box Score" of deaths and injuries were constantly with us—not unlike the listed deaths and wounded of area youth in the Korean War, published weekly in the *Pioneer Press* Sunday edition.

From Milwaukee to Minneapolis, the story was the same. A cursory search for "Milwaukee Road crashes" of a nearly one-hundred-year Winona newspaper database instantly yielded one thousand stories to review. Big town or small, it mattered not. From the 1901 crash at LaCrosse to the 1908 crash at Weaver with no air brakes to Milwaukee's home yard crash in 1927 causing the death of three and injury of four due to an "open switch" to the collision of a freight train and a "crack Milwaukee Road passenger train" in 1929, the headlines run into one another. Derailments, deaths and injuries of brakeman or fireman (or both) are documented. It was dangerous space where trains traveled, often leaving a "car sheared in half."

In Winona, we had crashes at Garfield Street (the death of a six-year-old boy) and Dacota and Laird and Winona and Chestnut Streets (and every street in between). Our twelve-year-old playmate died as he crawled under a boxcar that was "bumped ahead" in a neighborhood railroad yard. Observers watched from the train station platform on Center Street

Chicago NorthWestern Railroad Station, Winona, Minnesota, Huff and Second Streets, 1930s. *Courtesy Winona History Center.*

as a sixty-four-year-old resident living his life one hundred yards from the track ignored a train whistle, just to die within sight of his Winona Street home. In February 1954, there were two reported collisions within a two-hour period. In the first accident, a seventeen-year-old Minnesota City boy died at the Johnson Street crossing. The Box Score listed his truck's value at fifty dollars.

Our "home street" of Grand brought death to a Minnesota City man in May 1951, "the fifth crossing accident of this year." Progress of clearing the crash scene was "hampered by the presence of the large crowd." In the dark of a February supper hour of 1954 a few blocks away on my paper route, a housewife of the neighborhood had her auto pushed 160 feet by a train backing up at Dacota Street—all to earn herself "minor cuts and bruises." Auto-train crashes were grisly entertainment in our neighborhood.

An experienced, forty-year conductor of Milwaukee Road trains on these very rails during the heyday of open intersections was interviewed for this story. According to him, team members (engineer, conductor, head brakeman, rear brakeman and fireman) were constantly fearful of crashes as their trains passed through Winona in the 1960s. Larry reported:

> *We would literally hold our breath as we traveled through Winona. We could see stop signs being avoided, people darting across and accidents to come. Meeting of another train on the heavily used "double tracks" installed from St. Paul to Chicago increased the accidents. As one train went past in one direction, the hurried driver would cross onto the track—into the direct path of an oncoming train from the other direction!*

From the 1930s through the '70s, traffic was unbelievable. Nearly fifty trains per day (passenger and freights) passed over the tracks of the Milwaukee Road, Chicago and Northwestern, Burlington and Green Bay and Western near or through Winona. The numbers of trains of today are not known. Most intersections have been somewhat protected, although single-road entries in rural areas are still troublesome, as are drivers who choose to drive around controls and pedestrians who walk between stopped cars about to engage. The double track of our youth was removed throughout the "River Division" in 2005 with single track and computer-controlled long sidings taking its place.

THE HOBO: **HOMEWARD BOUND**

The freight trains didn't have windows, but they held a lot of interest. We saw people even closer, these riders of the rails—the hobos of America. Night and day they stood in the railcar doorway as trains passed by. Sometimes we would have a hobo or two drift down the street to someone's back door seeking a handout, but always in exchange for offered work. The hobo was one who was down and out but hadn't lost his pride. More than anything, he wanted to work and find a home. A bum was a bum. As the story from *Mulligan Stew* noted in "Growing Up on the Mississippi":

> *Hobos rode the rails into the heart of our small city along the Mississippi River—and into my heart.*
>
> *Daily arrival of freight trains in the 1940s and '50s brought us these open-air riders. Often seen standing in the open doors of the multitude of train cars passing through town, they sometimes chose to stop. Approaching a small home or two of the neighborhood after WWII, they entered or knocked on the screen door of the back porch, asking for a gift of a tomato from the garden, an apple from the tree or a sandwich to spare—and quietly inquired if there was any work they could do in exchange.*

H.L. Mencken in *The American Language* (1937) wrote:

> *Tramps and hobos are commonly lumped together, but see themselves as sharply differentiated. A hobo or bo is simply a migratory laborer; he may take some longish holidays, but sooner or later he returns to work. A tramp never works if it can be avoided; he simply travels. Apart from either is the bum, who neither works nor travels, save when propelled to motion by the police.*

Life as a hobo was dangerous. In addition to the problems of being itinerant, poor and far from home and support, plus the hostility of many train crews, they faced the railroads' security staff, nicknamed "bulls," who had a reputation of violence against trespassers. Moreover, riding on a freight train is dangerous in itself.

British poet W.H. Davies, author of *The Autobiography of a Super-Tramp*, lost a foot when he fell under the wheels when trying to jump aboard a train. It was easy to be trapped between cars, and one could freeze to death in bad weather.

The number of hobos increased greatly to an estimated 1 million or more during the Great Depression era of the 1930s. With no work and no prospects at home, many decided to travel for free by freight train and try their luck elsewhere. According to Ted Conover in *Rolling Nowhere* (1984), as many as 20,000 people were living a hobo life in North America. Modern freight trains are much faster and thus harder to ride than in the 1930s, but they can still be boarded in rail yards.

The Hobo Ethical Code of 1889 states in part, "Always try to find work, even if temporary, and always seek out jobs nobody wants. By doing so you not only help a business along, but ensure employment should you return to that town again. When no employment is available, make your own work by using your added talents at crafts."

Privately Operated Passenger Rail Service

The well-known Milwaukee Road servicing the Hiawatha Valley was chartered in 1847 as the Milwaukee & Waukesha Rail Road, with the name soon changed to the Milwaukee & Mississippi. It reached Waukesha in 1851, Madison in 1854 and Prairie du Chien in 1857. In 1858, the LaCrosse & Milwaukee Rail Road was completed between the cities of its name, reorganized in 1863 as the Milwaukee & St. Paul.

The "Milwaukee Road" acquired the St. Paul & Chicago in 1872, which had just completed a route down the west bank of the Mississippi from St. Paul to LaCrescent, opposite La Crosse, then a line from Milwaukee south to Chicago. A year later, it added "Chicago" to its name, creating the Chicago, Milwaukee & St. Paul Railway (CM&StP) in 1873.

From the mid-nineteenth century until approximately 1920, nearly all inter-city travelers in the United States moved by rail. The rails and the trains were owned and operated by private, for-profit organizations. Approximately sixty-five thousand railroad passenger cars operated in 1929. After 1920, passenger rail's popularity diminished. Rail passenger revenues declined dramatically between 1920 and 1934 because of the rise of the automobile, with many travelers lost to interstate bus companies such as Greyhound.

In the mid-1930s, railroads reignited popular imagination with service improvements and new, diesel-powered streamliners, such as the gleaming silver Burlington Zephyr and the steam-powered Milwaukee Twin Cities Hiawatha. Even with the improvements, on a relative basis, traffic continued to decline, and by 1940 railroads held 67 percent of passenger miles in the United States.

World War II broke the malaise. During the war, troop movements and restrictions on automobile fuel generated a sixfold increase in passenger traffic from its low point of the Great Depression. After the war, railroads rejuvenated overworked and neglected fleets with fast and often luxurious streamliners that inspired the last major resurgence in passenger rail travel.

The postwar resurgence was short-lived. In 1946, there remained 45 percent fewer passenger trains than in 1929, and the decline quickened. Passengers disappeared and so did trains. Few trains generated profits; most produced losses. Broad-based passenger rail deficits appeared as early as 1948, and by the mid-1950s, railroads were claiming aggregate annual losses on passenger services of more than $700 million (almost $5 billion in 2005 dollars).

By 1965, only ten thousand rail passenger cars were in operation, 85 percent fewer than in 1929. Passenger service was provided on only seventy-five thousand miles of track, a stark decline. The 1960s also saw the end of railway post office revenues, which had helped some of the remaining trains break even. Amtrak originated in 1971.

WINONA CONTINUES AS AN epicenter of railroads. Coal trains dominate. Amtrak is a whisper of its former self. The Grand Street I walked so many years ago is today one of the open, automatic-gated intersections of Winona. Those same tracks at Belleview Street remain, albeit protected. I can still stand on the same sidewalk and see Amtrak passengers pass in their daily journeys from St. Paul to Chicago, or the reverse.

More likely, I will be met in my now-drooping, waiting stance by massive freight trains that are hundreds of cars long—soon to be controlled by a single onboard railroad man and a computer control system one hundred or more miles distant.

The hobos are gone, frozen out by the speed of trains and the design of closed cars. Train crewmembers are virtually absent, with hardly anyone to whom we can wave. As the trains cruise through the night and shake the walls of Wayne's former bedroom, the beat goes on—as it did one hundred years ago.

I no longer live on Grand Street, but I am happy to report that safety at railroad intersections is a premier focus of railroad and city today.

Living yet with the fear of God, and of Engine no. 77052, kids still need to watch where they walk. Thankfully, the Box Score is no longer a published statistic.

As Amelia Wedemeyer reported in the *Winona Post* on May 5, 2014:

TRAIN AND VEHICLE COLLIDE; WINONA MAN INJURED

At 6:11 a.m. on Saturday, April 26, a Winona Police Department (WPD) officer in the area of Third and Ben streets heard a passing train applying its brakes. When he arrived at the train tracks at the intersection of Jackson and West Fifth streets, he noticed a vehicle that appeared to have been struck by a train. The vehicle had heavy damage to its right side. The driver of the vehicle, Jonathan Lott Freeman, 67, of Winona, appeared to be conscious and alert. Freeman, who said he had pain in his right leg, was the only individual inside the vehicle at the time of the accident. Freeman told the officer that he saw the railroad crossing with its lights on and its arms coming down, but he forgot that the tracks went diagonal through town and he thought he could make a left turn. An EMT arrived on the scene and Freeman was transported to a hospital for minor injuries. He was cited for failure to stop at a train signal.

Popeye's Legacy

FINDING A RESOURCE

I'm Popeye the sailor man
I live in a garbage can
I eats all the worms
And spits out the germs
I'm Popeye the sailor man
Toot! Toot!

Saturday and Sunday afternoons of the '50s were often spent at the West End Theater on Fifth Street of Winona. The "motion picture operators" gave us a whole plateful of westerns—for twelve cents each.

We saw Lash Larue, the Lone Ranger and Tonto, Tom Mix, Gene Autry, Hopalong Cassidy, Roy Rogers and his friend Dale Evens and so many more. The Sons of the Pioneers sang to us around the evening campfire.

The West End was a secondary outlet for movies. With musical blockbusters and epics like *Quo Vadis* occurring at the State Theatre downtown, we could get our fill of second-run movies at either the skinny Avon Theater on Third Street or the West End. With the West End closer to home and next door to the West End Confectionary ("the Confec")— run by Don and Audrey Ehmann in the 1940s and, in the 1950s, by Muriel Ehmke, who lived above the store—we could get a Cherry Coke or lime phosphate for a nickel in a conical paper cup with an accepting metal holder after a Tom Mix movie. We sometimes got an extra straw to share our bounty with a friend. It was terrific!

After the requisite newsreel and weekly dose of world news, war news and atomic blasts in the Nevada desert and before the "feature," Popeye showed up. *Popeye the Sailor Man* was a cartoon fictional character created by Elzie Crisler Segar. He appeared in comic strips and theatrical and television animated cartoons, with a first showing in the daily King Features comic strip *Thimble Theatre* on January 17, 1929.

In our cartoons of the 1950s, Popeye took on antagonists like the Sea Hag, blustering Bluto or Kazimoto of the mountains to inevitably face another of life's challenges. Once in a pickle and needing to rescue his girlfriend Olive Oyl or little Swee' Pea, he turned to his can of spinach for strength.

He was ever resilient and always on top of his game, introducing himself with the sparkling theme song "I'm Popeye the Sailor Man" by Sammy Lerner. Although Segar's *Thimble Theatre* strip was in its tenth year when Popeye made his debut, the sailor quickly became the main focus of the strip and one of King Features' most popular properties during the 1930s. The strip's title became *Popeye* in later years.

In every Popeye cartoon, the scrawny sailor is invariably put into what seems like a hopeless situation. After a beating by an antagonist, a can of spinach falls from inside his shirt or out of a back pocket, seemingly in endless supply. Popeye pops the can open with his remaining strength and immediately gulps the entire contents into his mouth. Sometimes he sucked the spinach in through his corncob pipe.

Upon swallowing the spinach, Popeye's body swelled and his physical strength immediately became superhuman. He easily saved the day and very often rescued others from a dire situation.

Popeye had a "go-to." His can of spinach was ever at the ready to get him through any travail. With his quaffing of a canful, swelled muscles allowed him to be victorious in any situation.

A TRANSFORMING ELIXIR

As kids, with our scrawny twelve-year-old bodies, there were moments in our lives when we could only wish for a transforming elixir like Popeye's spinach. We never really discussed Popeye. But this sailor who inevitably got into trouble, most often with his nemesis, Bluto, a well-remembered tough guy who inevitably wanted to pounce on someone, reminded us of our own troubles with a neighborhood bully down the street.

We wished for a Popeye or a Joe Palooka (another comic book character who had the ability to rescue) in our neighborhood. Cartoonist Ham Fisher saw Palooka as "a big, good-natured prize fighter who didn't like to fight." He was "a defender of little guys; a gentle knight." Joe Palooka exemplified sports heroes in an age when uprightness of character was supposed to matter most.

It's interesting that the lyrics of the *Popeye* theme song intersected with Palooka in one chorus of the song. He sang in the first cartoon, "I'm Popeye the Sailor Man/I'm one tough Gazookus/Which hates all Palookas." We saw both Popeye and Joe as "gentle knights and defenders of the little guy."

On occasion, we wished we could borrow Popeye's pipe, swing Larue's lash or use Zorro's sword to parry the onslaught and chase away the bad guys in our less-than-perfect lives. An old cockney saying suggested, "Life ain't all you want but it's all you got. Stick a flower in your hat and be 'appy."

We tried. As little kids, we found our way to school and to the playground. We even picked a flower on the way. We were 'appy and succeeded mostly, but we had moments of terror when a "tough guy" of the neighborhood threw rocks at us on our way home.

Loneliness after the passing of our mother was an endemic trait of the six kids. There was nowhere to go with the separateness we so felt. God abided and Pa provided, but we might have used a pat on the back or a big brother behind us when we faced our torment. That being said, big brother was a soft spot, a kind of tall, blond Palooka who gave us guidance, calmed our night sweats and softened our leg cramps.

Other torments and tormentors found us. In my life as a teenager, the occasion of a swelling cheek due to abscess of another tooth told me that it was time to visit the dentist again. I seldom visited the dentist—due to our absolute inability to afford it. When I visited Dr. Earsley, it seemed the outcome was always the same: another pulled tooth.

I often wondered how my teachers or coaches never noticed the swollen cheek or never quite found a way to rectify the situation of a motherless, striving child. Absent a supporter, I needed Popeye's spinach "go-to." As Steve Goodier said, "My scars remind me that I did indeed survive my deepest wounds. That in itself is an accomplishment. And they bring to mind something else, too. They remind me that the damage life has inflicted on me has, in many places, left me stronger and more resilient. What hurt me in the past has actually made me better equipped to face the present."

A TOOT FOR RESILIENCE

As young parents facing the challenges of raising children, we almost acquiesced to the Dr. Spock mentality of the times ("let it be"), but instead we held to common sense. Our "go-to" was the reality of knowledge gained from being raised in a workingman's environment. We rebounded from challenges. We simply worked harder and held a steady course. Years later, a child's temporary young adult abandonment of early family values gave wonder to it all.

Popeye reminds us that we all need to have a go-to. The problems of life continue to develop for each. We don't have spinach available and wonder what we are to do. Our good friend is out of town. We can't share with an adult friend. As Melissa Schubert has pondered, "Here's why I take comedies seriously: they present and celebrate the world in which we survive our own and others' mistakes, follies, transgressions and deep sins. However lightly, dimly, or bleakly, comedies revel in our survival—in the delaying of death and the staying of the curse. Comedies tell the story of ruined folk somehow avoiding ruin."

For our young family of the 1970s, Sunday nights with Lawrence Welk and his big-band television show provided a constant of grand music and a guise of harmonious family and community scenes that represented our expectations. His music strengthened us. His musical family was strong in offering "Just a Closer Walk with Thee."

Goodness was present in the simplicity of the orchestra's violin strains and in the simple expression of the North Dakota accordion player/band leader who said that life was "Wunnerful! Wunnerful!"

As life went on, all was not "wunnerful." There continued to be torments and tormentors of life. People occasionally threatened our well-being. In work and social settings, some "weak sisters" (male and female) outwardly or surreptitiously banded together to bully and threaten. Strength of character, belief and the can-of-spinach support of good people got us through the day. We needed resilience, to recover for another day.

Prayer life became expanded. Matthew Kelly in his book on spiritual renewal recently asked of us and offered: "When are we most fully alive? When we embrace a life of discipline. It sharpens the human senses. Discipline is the key to freedom. Freedom without discipline is impossible. [We need to continue to] stick to our guns" and focus on what is good, what is simple—and persevere.

Jeffrey Frye said, "Just because I face a defeat does not mean I am defeated."

We begin to build our supply of spinach. Today, we are afflicted with senior health issues and with the unintended loss of intimacy of our children as they find their way into parenthood and life's realities. We see the potential of living a diminished lifestyle.

Our "go-to" is God—and one another. We believe that God wants us to be happy. With our belief that He will sustain, we look ever forward to overcoming any adversity. He provides the spinach. He is our strength. As Kamal Ravikant said in *Live Your Truth*: "Success and failure come and go, but don't let them define you. It's who you are that matters…the most transformative experience has been the simple act of loving myself."

Popeye often said, "I yam what I Yam." And so for each of us. But being who we are says that we will forever need a "go-to"—a friend or resource with whom to share our travails.

> *I'm Popeye the sailor man*
> *I'm Popeye the sailor man*
> *I'm strong to the finish*
> *Cause I eats me spin-ach*
> *I'm Popeye the sailor man.*

The Circus Comes to Town

Somewhere there's a story about the circus coming to Winona. It needs to be told. As one who waited for the circus trains for hours in the dark of summer mornings in the 1950s, I can attest to the thrill, the anticipation of it all.

The arrival of the circus to Winona was an annual event for many of the years from 1870 through the 1950s. The circus of P.T. Barnum may have made it to Winona after Phineas Taylor started it in 1870, but there's no evidence. Most certainly the merged Barnum and Bailey Circus created in 1888 dropped by with eighty-five railroad cars. It was a circus then "taken to new heights" by James Bailey after Barnum's passing in 1891.

Under an "old rag carpet" borrowed from their mother, Marie, the Ringling boys of Baraboo, Wisconsin, started a penny circus in their backyard in 1874. Al, Otto, Alf, Charles and John showed early interest in the circus at their birthplace of McGregor, Iowa. In 1872, they moved to Prairie du Chien and on to Baraboo, where they founded their first commercial circus. Father August Ringling (from the German Ruengling) may have stopped off in Winona for a bit in the 1870s to work as harness maker, his second vocation after farming.

Brothers Gus and Henry joined the circus in the late 1880s. Sister Ida, the youngest, married Harry Whitestone North, who actually worked the rails for C&NW from Baraboo to Winona as his regular route. He was forty-four and Ida twenty-six when they married in 1902. Their sons John Ringling North and Henry Ringling North were second-generation leaders of the combined circuses.

Ringling Bros. announcement, prior to 1919 merger with Barnum & Bailey. *Courtesy Winona History Center.*

When the first-generation boys had gained eight dollars in Baraboo, they sewed a tent of sheeting, created a panorama on brown wallpaper and gained a Mexican pony to add to the family goat, fife, drum and Mom's plates. Soon they were drawing crowds and charging five cents.

A pony, the Ringlings' first circus horse, led the parade, performed in the ring and tossed off one or the other of the Ringling boys to add to the excitement. Some of Mom's plates broke when the boys did their plate spinning. It was one of the featured acts, with others including a goat act, a clown song, tumbling by the boys, fife and drum, a trapeze bar, bending through a hoop and more falling off the pony to bring good clean fun.

Their original (and long) name was "Ringling Brothers United Monster Shows, Great Double Circus, Royal European Menagerie, Museum, Caravan and Congress of Trained Animals." As the boys got older (ages fourteen to twenty-three), they took to the road with a wagon, three horses and the name "Ringling Brothers Classic and Comic Concert Co."

They visited the small towns of Wisconsin, performed a bit as a musical group at an opera house or two and created "entertainment of mirth and merriment." The boys gave "glorious processional amazement" in each of the villages in which they marched. In their single year together with experienced circus man "Yankee" Robinson, they learned from him that they must "keep moving." They also needed to create a reputation "strong and true." Yankee died within the year, but not before stating that the Ringlings were to become world circus leaders.

Within ten years, the five Ringling brothers had a full-fledged circus of 1,000 employees, 350 horses, chariots, 50 musicians, three large rings, "millions of yards of canvas" and four large trains of railroad cars, all to arrive in Winona on June 18, 1894. The Chicago and Milwaukee trains had left Mason City the night before and would head to Sparta upon completion of festivities in Winona.

The Ringlings insisted on cleaning up a bad reputation of some of the "hangers-on" who followed the circus—those creating disreputable and dishonest dealings. In the Ringling Circus, they banned the use of profanity. When the train arrived in Winona in 1894, there was a full-time superintendent of Pinkerton Detectives who cared for "style, morals and character of the show." As an editor of the Winona newspaper stated at the time, the story of the Ringlings "teems with lessons of patience, perseverance and honest effort." He suggested, "Alexander may have conquered the world, but the Ringling Bros. pleased it."

All were pleased with the show. The Ringling Bros. Route Book of 1894 states that the night house at Winona was "the largest night business in the State of Minnesota this year."

I wasn't there for the trains of 1894, but I did wait with the crowd in the early morning of July 26, 1951, to greet "The Greatest Show on Earth" as it arrived in all its glory. The combined shows of the early leaders had debuted in Madison Square Garden in 1919 as "Ringling Bros. and Barnum & Bailey Circus." In 1929, they added Sells-Floto, Hagenbeck-Walace, Robinson, Sparks, Buffalo Bill and the Al G. Barnes circuses to "own every traveling circus in America." Known worldwide for skill, thrill and integrity, they came to Winona. Wow!

The thrill was in being present for the arrival of the circus, to "hear the rumble of the incoming trains." It was *Music Man*, *Quo Vadis* and Frank Buck's *Bring 'Em Back Alive* animal adventure show all rolled into one at 5:00 a.m. on Second Street. And we could get up close and personal, as part of the "enhancement of the glorious procession." Once organized, we walked with performers and animals to the circus site at Goodview, some several miles west.

With animals, performers, trainers and a large gathering of parade observers along Fifth Street to cheer us on, we headed west to the opportunity of a morning's work setting up the tents and the potential of a free ticket for our effort. We longed to "see the wonder and astonishment of its circuses." How much could our scrawny preteen bodies help these seasoned veterans, their elephants and the choreographed construction of a mammoth city under golden tarps?

In "The Casual Observer," her regular column in the *Republican-Herald*, Gretchen Lamberton spoke wonderfully of the travel of elephants past the crowd on Broadway in 1949:

> As 23 elephants lumbered down the concrete street their big grey felt feet made a wonderful muted sound—"smish-smosh-smish-smosh-smish-smosh."…And the elephants—the lovely, shapeless, droll giants with their twinkling eyes and perpetual half-smiles. They stood in the animal tent swaying from foot to foot, spraying great trunkfuls of dirt over their backs. Sometimes they set down and let the dirt cascade blissfully down the vast slope of their backs.

She was there!

Once we were inside the "Big Top"—with balloons, cotton candy, pink lemonade and peanuts for elephants all in the hands of 4,500 patrons—the

Circus elephant at Winona, Minnesota. *Courtesy Winona History Center.*

ringmaster stepped forward in his tall hat; shiny and glorious long-waisted, star-spangled suit; and black leather boots. He was captured in shimmering glory in the spotlight. In the darkened tent, with drum rolls and slow, booming voice came his well-known words from center ring: "Ladies and gentlemen, children of all ages, welcome to the Greatest Show on Earth!"

It sent quivers down your spine—soon to see elephants and tigers and Lipizzaner horses in grand procession. The music stunned our senses. Trapeze artists would "fly through the air with the greatest of ease."

Emmett Kelly, the world's greatest clown, would bring his wandering "Weary Willie" appearance into view throughout the tents and into the crowd. He was joined by a cadre of clowns who unloaded from a single-seat car, as if a stuffed telephone booth of people were unloading.

A dwarf or two always joined the fray. Tigers stood on individual piers when a crack of the safari master's whip sent them from one place to another—with power, majestic beauty and obedience. Lipizzaners circled with bareback riders standing. Elephants abounded, rolled over, kneeled in place and soon raised stunning circus beauties perched on their heads to their full height. Oh the beauty of it all!

The ringmaster created the mood and energy. He led us through an ever-heightening process. With quiet, darkened lights and suspense, the raising of a cannon and a huge net on opposite sides of the tent—and *silence*—he brought us to the firing of the human missile (male or female) from the Zacchini Cannon. Invented by Ildebrando Zacchini in the 1920s after being inspired by Jules Verne, his "human cannonball" (son Hugo was the first) flew two hundred feet across the circus tent to land in the net and walk away. We could barely hold our seats as the cannon boomed and the flyer flew! The pace continued for two hours.

From a start in 1871, Winonans fell in love with the circus. Older's Circus appeared as "Museum, Circus and Menagerie" on June 17. With baby elephant, sea cow, gymnast, petrified giant and double-humped camels—all for fifty cents, twenty-five for children—activities were "enlivened by Prof. Good's New York Silver Cornet Band." The Great Trans-Atlantic Expedition appeared in 1873 with "500 living wild animals." Howe's Great London Circus came in 1876, 1879 and 1916 (Emmett Kelly joined them in 1920). Lent's New York Circus thrilled grandparents in 1876. Cole's brought its show in 1878 to the old circus grounds next to the Milwaukee Railroad tracks. Lemon Brothers came for a first time in 1895, following up in 1897, with Barnum and Bailey closely behind in the same year ("not being here for several years").

Many deserving mention include Hummell and Hamilton (1897), Gentry's (1900), Hagenbeck (1918, 1927 and 1935, to be absorbed by Ringling in 1935), Robbins Bros. (1928, 1930 at the West End Circus Grounds, with film star Buck Owens) and Sell-Floto bringing Tom Mix and his famous horse "Tony" to the show of 1930 at the West End fields, followed by Al G. Barnes Circus (1931) and Russell Bros. (1935). An indoor circus was held in 1941 at the Armory, conducted by Moneli Bros.

Clyde Beatty and his circus met the sheriff in 1948 at their grounds on Second and Liberty over some money owed to Olmstead County. The Shrine Circus at Gabrych Park of the same year featured "Big Bill" Bloomberg of Wabasha as ringmaster, with forty years in "nearly every noted circus." Dailey Bros. came to the old airport grounds with five rings in 1950.

Ringling Bros. Circus was a regular in 1893, 1894, 1896, 1899, 1904 and 1916—when it brought forty-seven railcars to town. The Sells Brothers were there to compete in 1894. The circus of 1896 brought a "crowd of bums," apparently attracted by the circus and crowds. Forthwith, they were locked up—all forty-one of them—until Tuesday. The police chief felt it best to "keep these hard characters in limbo."

The "Big One" for Winona was the combined Ringling Bros. shows, delighting "thousands of people in town" in 1926, 1937 ("27,000 attended!"), 1939, 1940, 1949, 1951 and 1954. "The Greatest Show on Earth" had made it to the greatest city of America. Its "streamlined show" of 1939 featured innovations of a new "Big Top," Caterpillar tractors instead of horses and air conditioning of the Big Top all under the direction of new leader John Ringling North. The thirty-six-year-old nephew of John Ringling greeted the folks at the circus site on East Sanborn and Jefferson.

Henry Ringling North, vice-president, stated in *Billboard* magazine that the greatest innovation came when he and John saw the Burlington railroad's bullet-like silver train (the Zephyr) at a crossing while in Winona. John declared, "Come next spring there will be no more Pullman coaches—the whole circus train will be silver." True to his word, the circus of 1940 arrived in Winona in the "streamlined train." Having worked with new designer Norman Bel Geddes over the winter, it "rained blueprints." His next promise was to bring air conditioning to the coaches of the train and "streamline all the flies out of the cookhouse." His brother offered that John's ambition to do the final act "seems a lot like trifling with the Almighty."

The show of 1949 arrived for its "first performance in Winona in ten years" from Madison, Wisconsin, with four trains and a total of eighty-nine cars. Included with the usual elephants, bareback equestrians and high-wire artists were "Clausson's Acrobatic Bears," for their first time in America. Did they know it was their first trip?

That 1949 show also brought Cecil B. DeMille, Hollywood's greatest director. He was observing and brainstorming for the $4 million *Greatest Show on Earth* movie that would open for Winonans at the State Theatre in 1952. Starring James Stewart as the clown, Cornel Wilde as a trapeze artist and Betty Hutton as an aerialist, the show was a big hit across the nation, in stunning Technicolor. DeMille stated of his weeklong visit on the circus tour, "The most amazing thing about this circus is the precision of production… it's precision, precision, precision."

The Greatest Show on Earth traveled the rails under the guidance of the Ringling Bros. A visit to its winter headquarters at Sarasota, Florida, allowed us to view the Ringling Mansion and Art Museum displaying a massive, worldwide collection of artifacts gathered by Mabel and John Nicholas Ringling. The busy state-owned museum, established in 1927, was left as a legacy by "one of the richest men in the world." It is the site of extravagance, opulence and abundance for all to see.

Circus clown
at West
Fifth Street,
Winona,
Minnesota.
Courtesy
Winona
History Center.

A separate Circus World museum was created in 1948 at Baraboo, Wisconsin, with banners, artifacts and history, including "The Wisconsin," John and Mabel's separate, private Pullman car built in 1905. On a recent visit to Circus World, we again felt the ringmaster's power and majesty in a sample performance in the original Ringling Bros. home tent. While standing in the darkened tent or outside next to original circus equipment and wheeled cages on the property, we were drawn back to another era.

The rails were taken up in 1956. The *Daily News* offered, "Ringling Circus Quits Big Top for Big Halls." The circus was sold, becoming wholly indoor. Emmett Kelly left the show to become mascot for the Brooklyn Dodgers, as well as television and night show entertainer. Under new ownership and direction of the Feld family since 1957, today's circus was alive and well until recent years, with an abundance of performances throughout the nation (searchable by zip code on its terrific website).

To be seen there were the Red Tour (Fully Charged), Blue Tour (Dragons) and Gold Tour (Barnum Bash). The closest performance for Winonans was to be in the United Center of Chicago, with twenty-one performances over a ten-day stand. To participate, we would need to ride the rails, reversing the process by going to the circus rather than having it come to us. The Dragons performance and its contested tribes offered all the "history of circus, with the promised addition of tribal myths and dragons" to create a new show.

However, due to social concerns by elephant rights activists, the elephants were sold. Shortly thereafter, the entire Ringling circus closed down in 2016.

It has been another very personal and memorable journey through the history and records of the Hiawatha Valley—a quest with new surprises, shared goodness and the excitement of the many for "Circus Day." I am delighted to have been a part of that history and the sensate pleasure shared in 1939 by an editor of the *Republican-Herald* when he opined:

> *When the sophisticated say, "When you've seen one circus, you've seen 'em all," they forget that the greatest appeal to visiting the big top year after year is the association of memories. Many a businessman today remembers when he toiled, a hot and dusty boy, carrying a bucket that sloshed water on his trousers, to earn a free ticket from the elephant-keeper. His sense of enjoyment is no less keen when he sees the circus today, even though the elephants now quench their thirst from a motor-driven water wagon.*

Wish to see you in the Big Top for the Greatest Show on Earth.

A Day on the River

OLE, BAD BOYS AND BOATHOUSES

The twenty-five-horsepower Evinrude motor hung on the back of the wood strake, lap-sided sixteen-foot "power boat." It was all we needed for a day of fun on the river in the 1950s. Housed in Everett's shanty boathouse at the foot of Olmstead Street on the Mississippi River, the boathouse was the place from which we teenagers could take off (with Everett's permission) for an afternoon of water skiing along the sand islands of the river.

We dodged towboats and raced on wood skis behind and across the minor wake of the sixteen-footer, but occasionally we powered up behind bigger boats—like an eighteen-footer with a thirty-five. No way were we going to keep up with Russ Rossi's record of pulling up eight water skiers at the same time with his V-8 ski boat.

Neither were we about to mount and tumble off the front of the ten-foot-high water ski jump constructed off the main channel of the river by and for members of the local waterskiing club. That took horsepower and guts. Whether behind big boat or small, we loved our time on the river. On a singular and special summer afternoon, I was able to get my girl up on water skis behind her father Fred's fourteen-footer—with a mere ten-horse Johnson offering a more sedate ride.

Along with a dozen others, Everett's squatter's shack was a permanent fixture on the river at Olmstead Street. Resting on used and emptied fifty-gallon metal drums, it rode out the ravages of winter, rose to the skies with spring flooding and accommodated all manner of human and natural visitors in the carefree days of summer.

Backwater boathouses on the Mississippi River at Winona, Minnesota. *Courtesy Winona History Center.*

The one who rode the river for the longest time at the foot of Olmstead was Clarence Gorr, eventually dubbed the "mayor" of the small riverside community. He lived there (free) year-round for forty years, starting in 1912. In 1928, the game warden presented him with a search warrant the day before the opening of muskrat season. Word must have come down that Clarence was out chasing muskrats before the season, for he was found out and fined fifty dollars "for possession of muskrat skins out of season—a willful violation," according to the *Winona Republican-Herald*.

A neighbor of his, commercial fisherman Julian Laska, was there long enough to build a five-room floating structure for his wife and three children. For all, maintenance was minimal, with replacement of drums a singular necessity so as not to sink into the channel. As the barrels rusted out or split from winter freeze, each leaking barrel was replaced by an Everett or a Julian, or combination of neighbors working together. With a homemade two-by-four structure fitted around a new barrel, the new barrel was pried into place under the boathouse side by superhuman effort—"popping" the new barrel into place.

One who was there in the 1950s offered:

We had an "h-looking jig." The barrel went in the u-shaped part and we hooked that under the house and pushed down on the leg part of the "h." The barrel would slip out of the jig and under the house. How does that sound?

The old, rusted hulk of barrel was often easier to remove than the insert. Since it had taken on water, it could usually be pushed out of the way by a boy or two swimming around the wooden framed structure. The new barrel was full of air, and it was a serious challenge to push underwater and into place.

My teenage girlfriend and eventual wife's father, Fred, had a cool nineteen-foot, mahogany Trojan DayCruiser. With twin Johnson thirty-fives, it rested on days off in an updated and large boathouse that he owned located at the Winona Boat Club Harbor, down the road and behind the bathhouse. Just off vestiges of the old High Wagon Bridge that crossed to Winona before the turn of the century, the harbor was an organized and official grouping of well-built shanties—with bylaws, a "work committee" and an elected Commodore.

With several dozen members and boathouses; a floating walkway fronting them all; an annual luau; an ice fishing contest; and formalized, electrified and private membership, members were still squatters on someone else's property—in the fashion of boathouses up and down the river. Latsch Island and its surrounds, their area of residence, had been donated to the City of Winona by John Latsch in the early 1900s. It was to be held in a natural state for eternity. The boathouse environment constituted natural, it seems.

Inside Fred's boathouse was an open water space for the boat surrounded by a several-foot walkway holding boating necessities, a charcoal grill, gas storage and a small refrigerator for beer and pop—necessities for hot days on the river. Overhead was a chain and winch to hoist the boat out of the water for repairs and winter storage.

We spent our moments around and about boathouses such as these from earliest days. As schoolboys on a lark in winter, we sometimes visited them (without owner permission) looking for fun and adventure. Some of the boys vandalized and stole items from boathouses over the years. Four of my Madison School fifth-grade friends soaked a boathouse floor in December 1951 with kerosene, lit a match and burned a boathouse down, causing $300 in damage. They were, obviously, "referred to juvenile authorities."

An "ax-wielding ten-year-old" caused havoc "for some time" with boats and boathouses as he attacked them in 1944. He was caught in December and also "referred to juvenile authorities."

Fishing tackle was stolen at a boathouse on Olmstead Street in 1943, on the Hamilton Street harbor in May 1947 (tools and tackle) and on Kansas Street, where youths used "submarine tactics" to steal fishing tackle and field glasses. Three youths were arrested for having swum under the boathouse to enter and steal goods. On nearby East Front Street in 1937, a man lost his one-hundred-pound anchor, with an additional twenty-five pounds of sausage swiped off a nearby parked railroad refrigerator car by the same well-muscled youth. Four youth were "nabbed in burglary at the foot of Ewing Street" in 1952 with a stolen shotgun and boots—possibly some of my Madison School classmates.

At the Lake Winona boathouse of Hilet Hajicek (star player of the Winona Hornets hockey team), someone jimmied the window in April 1945. Latsch Island saw assault in May 1951 by visitors (obviously the aforementioned youth), who stole soft drinks and $2.75. But did they return the bottles?

Some thieves took larger items—like the whole boathouse! The game warden lost his forty-by-ten-foot float in November 1934 (for either spite or as a prank), to be found "in willow growth near the Burlington [Railroad] Bridge." Investigating detective George Fort (former motorcycle officer of the Winona Police Department) was credited with the save—probably propelling him into his new job as sheriff of Winona County.

Jim Hauser of the Mertes Boat Livery across the bridge had boats, motors and boathouse stolen in one fell swoop in October 1953 after some axe-wielding character cut the metal mooring cables. With a dozen police and county officials searching, they found the boathouse a half mile downstream near Bathhouse Slough. What a ride!

It was big business for boathouse rentals and boat and motor sales in the late 1940s and '50s. Evinrude and Alto motors, Dunphy (100th Anniversary Year, 1954) and Century boats were a few of the featured items at Central Motor Company on Market Street. Gasoline cost 23.9 cents per gallon in 1950, moving to 25.5 cents by 1952.

Jay Mertes of Winona serviced them all (Evinrude, Johnson, Mercury and Sears) at his shop at 75 West Second Street and at his small service and dockage area on the bridge road to Wisconsin. He lived kitty-corner across King and Harriet Streets from Paul Pletke, local grocer renowned for servicing crews of towboats of the Mississippi, as well as the occasional boathouse or houseboat.

Ole, Jay and Paul were true originals to the river and the boathouse scene. Before the outboards of Ole, the launches of Youmans, Foster (a twenty-five footer), Mitchell and others were "lifted above the water line" in November

OLE EVINRUDE BROUGHT US THE BOATHOUSE

Originally Ole Andreassen Aaslundeie of Norway, he settled in Cambridge, Wisconsin (where he chose the name Evinrude after his mother's Norwegian farm), and went on to Madison at age sixteen to become a machinist.

With his wife, Beth, since she was sixteen, they had a partnership and love affair with boats and each other. His rowboat trip across Okauchee Lake in Wisconsin in the summer of 1906—for ice cream and the resultant meltdown of same—caused him to create the outboard motor.

Beth was there as advertising manager and guide when he invented the first outboard motor in 1907 and when he refined it into the ELTO (Evinrude Light Twin Outboard) in 1919—a "more efficient and lighter two cylinder." Extremely successful in his own right, Ole allowed two motorcycle guys (Harley and Davidson) to "tinker in his machine shop."

Ole's Evinrude Motor Company later merged with Stephen Briggs of Briggs & Stratton to form a new company, ultimately becoming OMC and joining the Bombardier stable in Canada alongside Johnson Motors and Ski-Doo snowmobiles.

From personal research by the author, with assist from Bob Matson, author of What's In Your Boathouse.

1901. It was reported in the *Republican-Herald* that "in general figures it can be said that a yacht uses a pint of gasoline an hour for each horsepower of its engine. In the main, the measure holds good."

In 1903, the clam diggers of the Mississippi were looking forward to another successful season of gathering shells and pearls for resale to button manufacturers and jewelers. Getting ready, they were constructing a boathouse with a "boom" of heavy logs as their boathouse base. That same year in May, Steve Ward's boathouse was "bound to get under water before he can get a chance to repair it," and "Edw. Roessner purchased from Wm.

Blair for $200.00 his huge launch boathouse." George Fischer's boathouse was stolen and ended up across the channel in Wisconsin in 1905, to be found without George's two rowboats.

In 1906, a headline noted, "Boathouse Burglars Are Sent to State Penitentiary" for theft. One received a one-year, six-month sentence. The other received a one-year, three-month sentence. September 1915 saw Soren E. Sorenson, LaCrosse chief train dispatcher for the Milwaukee Road, "Set River on Fire." He dumped water and oil out of his boat and "shortly after threw a cigar stub into the river." The oil ignited, and "the house and launch were a mass of flames. Two other parties ran thru sheets of fire and were badly burned. Sorenson dove out from under the boathouse to safety only after receiving frightful burns from which he now suffers." The boathouse "had already burned to the water's edge." Boathouse builders in LaCrosse in 1916 discovered the body of a six-year-old under their construction site.

Drownings (and rescues) were prevalent along the river near and far, with losses at boathouses continuing at Kansas Street, Hamilton, Bathhouse Slough and Lake Winona. The sad loss of a four-and-a-half-year-old boy through the ice in 1954 was a real tragedy. In the drowning of four young people (two male, two female) who hit his "projected boathouse" near his property off LaMoille, E.L. King (owner of J.R. Watkins Company) was sued in 1917 for damages. The charges were dismissed.

A more fortunate twelve-year-old was rescued in 1941 at the foot of Kansas Street on the river when he became entangled in a setline. He was more afraid than thankful when he offered, "My mother won't like it that I got my pants wet."

The city levee on Main Street had a boathouse settlement by 1906. Two men were sent to municipal court for "removing articles from boathouses." These same boathouses drew the ire of residents of the city when squatters there erected "Private Docks" signs. R.J. Fujina, president of River Sand and Gravel in 1916, opposed the action when these people "anchored to the city's levee wall and monopolized the entire space." The city must have taken matters into hand, for by 1943 they had offered a contract to re-shingle the city's boathouse there.

On the other end of Main Street on the lake was the boathouse of A. Ward, where he held an "Open Air Prayer Meeting" in 1899. With several iterations of both city and resident boathouses, the city's boathouse on the lake evolved. A $15,000 boathouse owned and operated by the City Park Commission was in place for a November 1924 opening.

The Clark brothers, well-known Winona insurance operatives in later years, operated the city-owned facility as boys in 1927, with rentals and concessions. By city declaration, the non-floating boathouse and winter warming house was to have "not less than twenty rowboats for rent, not less than five canoes for rent." In addition, there was to be rental storage space for an additional sixty canoes and skiffs.

During ice skating season, all the boats were removed. Operating hours of the warming house we so often visited were from 8:00 a.m. to 11:00 p.m. on weekends and 1:00 p.m. to 11:00 p.m. on other days. Throughout the year, it became the meeting place for fun, for Brownie Scouts, Jr. Optimist Archers, Girl Scouts, an occasional reading of the *Velveteen Rabbit* and singing of the "good night song." Today, we know it as the Lake Winona Shelter across from the bandshell.

Howard W. Clark went on to become Commodore of the Winona Motorboat Club at the foot of Kansas Street for a dozen years. In his official photo in 1941, he was shown in his *"cheminot nationale"* uniform—of the board of directors of the 40 & 8. Not forgetting their roots, Clark & Clark Insurance provided liability coverage for the city boathouse in 1954 and beyond.

Other forces were at work to cause damage and loss to boathouses up and down the river—beyond Winona's errant youth who passed through the generations. In March 1919, a series of boathouses lashed together were "under perilous condition'" in the middle of the river—having floated away in the high waters of March—along with "boats, boathouses and accessories."

John Palubicki, local fireman, in 1920 lost his launch house when five launch houses were loosened and adrift. They struck the NW Railway Bridge "with considerable force." John reported that "it cost him some eighty dollars in the first place."

The high river and ice jam at Bay State Milling Company on March 29, 1929, "took boathouses and houseboats with it." In addition, "Rain has honeycombed the ice and there was little chance of saving the string of boathouses in the channel. Four boats were rescued, with fourteen yet tied up in the ice." They drifted to Blacksmith's Slough across from Homer. Max Conrad's boathouse was one of those damaged.

According to the Winona Newspaper Project, "Winona's river colony, a group of about a dozen houseboats, was nearly submerged today—and another rise of a foot in the stage of the water will drive them into tents and higher ground."

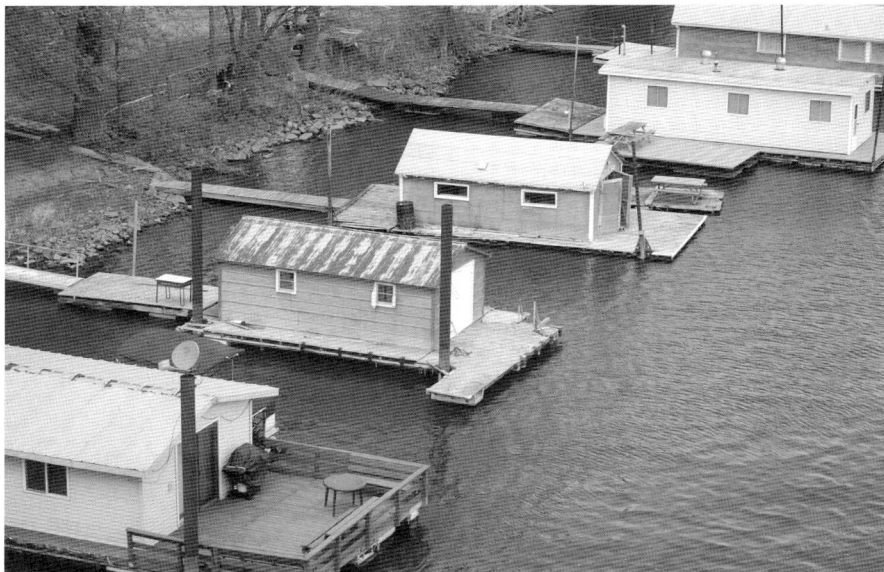

Boathouses south of Winona, Minnesota, on the Mississippi River, 2018. *Author's collection.*

The "Voice of the Outdoors" column of the *Republican-Herald* reported that a January 1944 five- to eight-foot drawdown of the river created "much damage wrought to installations along the river," including Bathhouse Slough (behind the bathing beach). In May of that year, a property dispute caused an owner of a boathouse at Minnesota City to have a bonfire. "The man who set fire to his own boathouse was freed by the sheriff." Maybe he was just making room for those on Olmstead Street, as the Winona Newspaper Project noted:

> *A different threat came to the owners of boathouses at the Olmstead Street footing—with realities of needed flood protection of the city and with government directive. An August 1952 newspaper announced, "Riverfront Residents Lose Homesites. The eighteen boathouses and dozen houseboats of the dockage are to be wiped out by proposed dike construction"—forcing owners to seek new locations.*
>
> *They had been pre-warned in 1949 when the NW Railway wrote to the city council informing that they were about to "take steps to oust squatters" on their mile and one-half property northwest of Winona Street. "Sixty-eight or more of boathouses, shack-type dwellings, encroachments, etc."*

were cited, especially at Olmstead Street. "All houseboats and boathouses have been dismantled or moved," reported Capt. Frank Fujina in his "Ol' Man River" newspaper column.

"The (afore-mentioned) mayor sat on an overturned barrel and watched his erstwhile bailiwick being ground out of existence by dragline and bulldozer" on September 11, 1952. At age 78, with eviction notice in hand, the "mayor" moved to a room at a downtown hotel.

R.D. Whittaker founded Whittaker Marine and Manufacturing at 24 Laird Street in Winona in 1954. He created a series of seven houseboats that sold for between $12,000 and $30,000 each. Forty to fifty feet in length, they plied the rivers in good order, with several bringing fifty numismatists (coin collectors) to Blackbird Island for a steak fry in 1957. The "Picture of the Year" in the *Daily News* was of Mayor Rudy Ellings pulling up five waterskiers with his Whitcraft. The company sold to Rockwell International in 1969, closing in 1972, with property sold to Winona Industries.

There is a whole other story yet to be told of teenage parties and midnight romances along the river sand islands—a province of young and old. A dozen

Typical houseboat of the 1960s, housed alongside boathouses on the river at Winona, Minnesota. They were self-powered. Local fun and dancing onboard often featuring the band The Ferraris. *Courtesy Winona History Center.*

of Winona's community leaders were featured in a January 1952 *Republican-Herald*, Merritt Kelley–photographed story of "the latest social fad of fishing parties held in an empty boathouse." With cocktail party, steak fry, heated house and "all the comforts of home," many drilled holes and fished (on occasion). Teenagers chose not to have their pictures taken, but images and memories have been indelibly captured forever.

Any excuse summer or winter, young or old, brought the best of social activity and "moments to remember" to Winona's boathouses. Some fished. Some waterskied. Some watched the sunset. All loved their moments on the river.

In his recent book, Bob Matson brought us full circle back to boathouse origins and restored boats in his musings:

> *The paint is dry and peeled, the windows cracked.*
> *Propped up by logs, it leans slightly to the back.*
> *The morning sunlight streams in through the door,*
> *Illuminating the memories a lifetime spent in store…*
> *In time honored tradition it holds guard in this way;*
> *Always gazing quietly over our corner of the bay.*

One who was there offered on the website You Know You're in Winona If…, "You've been to a boathouse party in summer, winter, spring and fall—and never got wet!" Another sage of the time suggested, "You could have a lot of fun atop those barrels."

Warm Delights

A REFLECTION

I can still see the snow against the high overhead light. It was in the center of the neighborhood park crossed on the diagonal sidewalk on my way home from the Y, from basketball practice or another early teenage night out in the 1950s. There hung a single, shrouded light bulb in the center intersection of the park. Approaching, it seemed that the air about it suddenly had become warmer. It may have been the coldest of nights, but the single lamp with its metal downward reflector caused a radiance both welcoming and enthralling.

As I walked the sidewalks of our valley town in winter, there was no underwear that I remember adding to my skinny legs to offer an extra layer of warmth. There were just the worn, tattered J.C. Penney underwear briefs worn day and night and washed out in our Saturday morning kitchen and temporary laundry on "wash day."

Warmth was a key to our survival in winter. We hustled from place to place on cold Minnesota days toward the warmth of school classrooms and teachers, YMCA, library, church or Grandma's house. Nothing was more exciting than arriving home to the warmth of our little house on Grand Street.

Being truly "snug as a bug in a rug," I survived each night in my used U.S. Army bunk bed with its tattered quilt requiring careful arranging so as not to have an open hole. My attic bedroom window had ice on it many mornings. Moving quickly downstairs on the way to the bathroom for a splash and rinse on a dark winter morning, a twist of the lower crank of the wood stove was made and wood pieces were added to our potbellied stove in the middle room. The first riser among seven (Pa and six kids) in our house ignited the day's heat source from coals nesting therein.

On Saturday, a brother or two and I would set up in the kitchen the wash tubs that hung in the small outside back porch. We would fill them from the single cold-water spigot of the sink and heat some water on the kitchen stove to be added to the wringer washer, also kept on the back porch, beside the stacked firewood. With suds and throbbing of the old Maytag electric motor, the work and power of men (boys) and machine was in process.

Some warm water was added to the first tub (first rinse) where roughened clothes were first squeezed through the wringer. Then on to the second tub—a cold-water, hand-dipped rinse—squeezed again by the wringer and headed for the clothesline. The warmth of the kitchen came as a combination of our hard work and the blessed fire of our kitchen range.

As eight- and ten-year-olds, we twisted and squeezed and kept our fingers out of the wringer's rollers. Pushing the lever, we rotated the rollers from

1952 McCullough chainsaw, author owned and utilized, with wood supply headed for home heating in 1980s. *Author's collection.*

washer to first tub, to between first and second tubs and then, again, to squeeze the final product out into an awaiting wicker basket carried off by scrawny arms for hanging.

We hung wet clothes either indoors or outdoors depending on weather. Indoors, the clothesline was strung in the middle room, sometimes accommodating frozen shirts and pants that we had started outdoors on cold winter days. There were times when Pa was flush and we would have the Winona Wet Wash man pick up and deliver our cleaned, wet clothes ready for hanging. Oh they smelled so clean, so fresh!

My friend Wayne's house was not so different from ours in design or function. There were five kids and parents tucked into a small three-room house. The four boys were set up in a separate summer kitchen-like, add-on room that had its own separate entrance. To get to the kitchen, dining room or bathroom (a single space with the bare essentials) of the small main house, you stepped outside the bedroom and across a wood platform to enter the home's hot kitchen. The main difference between Wayne's house and ours was that his mom was home all day to "keep the home fires burning."

Their small Belleview Street home was always warm and welcoming, with a continuous pot of hot coffee on the stove for after-school kids, parents and guests. Mom was always in the kitchen baking or preparing wildlife brought home by hunter Donald and his boys—exquisite dinners. The oil stove in the middle room radiated heat throughout the small home. A kerosene-fired stove constantly heated the brothers' annex, keeping the timber-like cabin warm and the indoor air oil pungent.

We stayed warm at home with the heat from our two wood stoves—the central middle room potbelly and the range in the semi-large kitchen. The kitchen range was for cooking, heating the room and the water in a copper boiler for wash day and Saturday evening kitchen "baths." We had neither bathtub nor shower, which would have necessitated a gas-fired hot water heater.

When I was about ten or so, we gained the hot water heater, shower and a bathtub for sister upstairs as Pa remodeled our attic into bedrooms, updated the small home's electricity and plumbing and put an oil stove in the middle room. The small metal shower in our equally small downstairs bathroom was a new treat for Pa and the boys. These were essentials for our family, but they were certainly not within his budget. Somehow he borrowed the money—in spite of his lack of income—to make spaces for us all.

The crossover times of cool spring days and cooler fall days kept us in a tattered (yet clean) overlay of shirts and jacket. There was no thermostat on the wall. We hustled up a quick rinse of our face in the single bathroom and headed off to school to the adorable warmth of our teachers and classrooms. As the days cooled down into night, Pa would keep a warm fire going and offer a hot supper of pork chops or goulash or buckwheat pancakes—and the cycle continued.

Winter Friday nights and Saturdays and Sunday afternoons found us on the local ice skating rinks and in the city's toasty warming houses. Whether wood-fired potbelly heat or overhead gas blower, we were enticed by the warmth and the camaraderie.

From kindergarten to marriage, I was warmed by the presence of girlfriends. They always brought a warm feeling with their near presence on a kindergarten mat or even nearer in the back seat of a borrowed automobile as we "double-dated" and snuggled to watch a movie at the Sky-Vu Drive-In. The darkened balcony of the State Theatre across from the Varsity Inn was the site of a stolen first kiss, definitely a "warm" moment.

We gave a valentine from the twenty-nine-cent package and a few special, hand-selected candy hearts to our sweetheart in elementary school. In junior high and high school and all across the classrooms, notes were passed. In hallways, study hall or Latin class, we were warmed by a girlfriend's cursive writing style and excited by the received and meaningful message. We sometimes read between the lines for an added message.

Today, as I ventured out at 5:00 a.m. on a pre-winter morn, I felt the chill of winter on me. I left behind momentarily all the controls and comforts of home, including an ever-available hot shower. The instant heat in home and car are there on coldest of days. We even have electric blankets to add additional heat as we sit in a cool corner or snuggle down for a long winter's nap.

I don't have to get out the crank to start a heater-less 1934 Plymouth coupe as Pa did. His first "family car" was gained when I was ten or so. Most generally, the city bus served Pa's needs and our own as we headed off for Grandma's day care for littler ones in the east end of town. Today, I have toasty-warmed electric seats in my luxury car.

The warmth of today is internal. I am warmed by the memories and accomplishments over all the years. Every day, after sixty years, my childhood sweetheart is yet at my side. We have accomplished much together. Occasionally, I make her a homemade valentine, lay out a few selected candy heart messages next to her coffee cup or give her a hug in our thermostatically controlled and toasty kitchen. On a big day, I may even pop for a dozen roses.

Remembrance of a warm memory, family photo, 1940s. *Author's collection.*

As we look out on our lakeside backyard on a snowy night, an overhead light reflects our shared memories and enduring mutual love. The personal warmth I felt from the small park's overhead light when I crossed the diagonal so many years ago is felt yet today.

It has been a satisfying trip to have lived in the heart of the Hiawatha Valley.

The Hot Fish Shop

Good Friends, Good Food and Good Fishing

The Mississippi, with more than 150 different kinds of fish
is the collector's gold mine.
—*Lefty Himes,* Voice of the Outdoors, *1964*

Fish surrounded us. Our home, after all, was on the Mississippi River. In our backyard were pickerel, walleye, sunfish, northern pike, dogfish, crappie, bass, catfish and carp. One could only imagine the extent of stock and supply of fish to the American Indians who preceded us on these sand prairies. As Captain Orrin Smith (founder of Winona) noted, reflecting in 1915 on his boyhood days along the river:

> During the writer's boyhood day, fishing was largely done from rafts tied along the riverfront. We caught many nice bass and pike of good size, to say nothing of pickerel, suckers, red-horse, sturgeon, sunfish and catfish. On the Wisconsin side, the sloughs over there were then navigable and almost alive with fish.…Dozens of Indians came every day of summer from the Wisconsin side of the river, bringing their canoes, game and fur skins.

As multitudes of Europeans came to settle in Winona, they brought their own experiences with fish and its part in necessary, daily sustenance. Grandparents had come from within miles of the Baltic Sea. A great-grandfather had traversed the world as a ship's captain out of Stetin, bringing back treasures of the sea. Fish was in our bones.

One of the first advertisers of "Fish for Sale" and first to greet early settlers stepping off the steamboat in Winona in 1871 was the Owens and Beyerstedt Groceries and Provisions Store at Second and Main, opposite the steamboat landing. There were many others who lined the sandy streets of the Mississippi shoreline offering fresh, dried and smoked fish, a staple of the day and the region.

Available at Owens and Beyerstedt were staples, groceries, apples, oysters, salt fish, hams, dried beef and trout. Chas. Deering at 121 West Third Street offered Lake Superior trout, whitefish and other fish every Friday in 1889. By 1895, John Winkels was offering the same at Second and Lafayette Streets. In 1900, F.G. Vila was at 103 West Third Street offering "FISH," with whitefish and catfish also available a block over at Ramm's Market on Center Street (1901).

In 1915, Skoglun's Market offered fresh carp and sunfish at 519 Huff (phone 493). Ziegenfuss Bros. offered "Fresh Fish—Pike and Pickerel" at phone number 287 in 1921.

FISH WAS IN OUR BONES AND OUR HERITAGE

For all the years, fish were available in the river, the adjoining sloughs and in the creeks of the valleys. We harvested for fun and food. That harvesting and consuming of seafood is an ancient practice dating back at least forty thousand years. Analysis of skeletal remains of Tianyuan man of eastern Asia showed that he regularly consumed freshwater fish. Discarded fish bones and cave paintings show that such foodstuffs were historically important for survival and consumed in significant quantities.

People lived as hunter-gatherers and were constantly on the move. As with Wah-Pa-Sha's Prairie, permanent settlements most often were near food sources, including fish. We were thrilled with God's largesse in such a beautiful surround.

Only a few blocks away from the river at Mankato Avenue and East Wabasha Street was the home of Henry Kowalewski. Born in 1889 in Winona to Mr. and Mrs. Joseph Kowalewski, he joined five brothers and three sisters. He finished his schooling at St. Stan's Notre Dame and proceeded to spend "several years as a soldier of fortune—venturing from the East Coast to the Pacific Coast."

He returned home to show himself as one of "a family interested in dramatic work" with a Winona Opera House role in the production of *In Bad*, and other musical reviews of 1922. He was the experienced "Minstrel Lead" in a 1933 production. He was meant, however, to spend his life as a person feeding the masses with his fish and talents.

Incorporated in 1920 in Winona, the Northwestern Fish Company of New York opened at 50 East Second Street with M.N. Lipinski as secretary-treasurer. Dave Gantenbein, "pioneer fisherman" of Diamond Bluff, Wisconsin, and Lipinski would lead the company, with both "having been engaged in commercial fishing for many years."

Northwestern shipped carp to New York via special cars in late fall and winter. Henry was hired to be the New York representative, serving from 1919 to 1924. Fish were caught on the Mississippi and held in storage ponds (up to 1 million fish) until the best time for taste and shipping. Notably, the Maiden Rock Pond of 1924 was representative of holding ponds where Northwestern fed carp cracked corn.

Henry said at the time, "Carp are looked upon as not a very good fish. This is because people usually catch and eat them in spring, when fish are spawning and in poor condition. They would not know the same fish if caught late in the fall when it is in top condition and ready for the market."

Nearly one hundred years later, a *Big River* magazine article of 2004 reported, "Carp are safer to eat than many game fish. The carp eat mollusks, insect larvae and some vegetation; thus absorbing fewer toxins."

After gathering millions of carp and shipping them east, Henry, the former deputy county auditor and recent NW Fish Company employee, decided in 1926 to run for state representative. His home was yet at 703 East Wabasha, with parents and brother Vincent next door at number 707. With his parents he soon founded the Standard Fish Market.

Henry and Vincent are shown as operators of Standard Fish at 771 East Wabasha in 1931. Listed as wholesalers of fish, they sold catfish, pike, bullheads, smoked carp and smoked sturgeon. "We deliver (phone 5002)."

Carp broth was often served in the Czech and Polish homes of east Winona at Christmas. Along with kielbasa (dozens of varieties of sausage, a staple of Polish cuisine), boiled potatoes, warm beet salad, pickled pig's feet and czemina (duck blood soup), there was zupa Rybna, or fish soup. Central to the dinner was Ryba smażona, the delicate, breaded and fried fish fillet that preceded the batter-fried pike of Henry's soon-to-be Hot Fish Shop.

Other delicacies proposed by customers of Winona's Bud Ramer Fish Company in the aforementioned *Big River* magazine included deviled carp, carp dumplings, carp aux raisins, buttermilk fried carp fillets, carp tacos and carp casserole.

At 351 Mankato, on an adjacent corner to the fish market on Wabasha Street, was a restaurant run in 1931 by Edw. Gallas. Henry took over the restaurant in his backyard that same year to operate it in conjunction with his fish market. "The founder and president" of the Hot Fish Shop on Mankato Avenue, he served the batter-fried fish that he "learned to like in St. Louis." He served both catfish and pike. The evening meal on the opening of Christmas Eve 1931 consisted of shrimp salad, two pike fillets, cabbage salad and French fries—for thirty-five cents!

Closing his original site in 1934 due to construction of the Washington-Kosciusko School on the block-long property, the move allowed him to build anew. He placed himself front and center at the intersection of Highway 14/61/43 and the Mankato Dike Road—at Henry's proclaimed "Gateway to Nation's Summer Playground, Winona, Minnesota."

In 1933, a Hot Fish Shop ad of 351 Mankato (across the street from Sam Joswick's Groceries and Meats) read, "A Light Summer Food with a Glass of Cold Beer." The cold beer "chaser" was a tradition continued with the opening of the new Hot Fish Shop on December 29, 1934, in the shadow of Sugar Loaf and the very local Bub's Brewery. It was reported by locals out for their noon business lunch well into the 1980s that "one couldn't have a walleye lunch at the Hot Fish Shop without a cold Bub's Beer."

As the new shop and fish market business grew "at the gateway" this side of Sugar Loaf, it gained a national audience. The Hot Fish Shop Highway 14/61 entrance to Winona intercepted nearly every vehicle traveling between Chicago and Minneapolis.

To further the cause, Henry conducted a nationwide postcard campaign (one-cent stamp!) to customers who had stopped by. Each was sent a beautiful colored print of a white-bricked, red-roofed Hot Fish Shop. The card announced, "Popular Restaurant of the Northwest," further showing it to be "in the Shadow of Sugar Loaf along the Scenic Mississippi, Featuring

Nationally acclaimed, the Hot Fish Shop stood at the junction of Highways 14, 61 and 43 at the entrance to the Hiawatha Valley. *Courtesy Winona History Center.*

Boneless Pike, Seasonal Fish and Seafood—endorsed by Duncan Hines." The steaming batter-fried walleyed-pike luncheon was the top seller for many years (to 75 percent of the customers), served with the greatest homemade tartar sauce ever made.

Alphonse "Mose" Bambenek was head chef and Henry's nephew. For all the years, he was at Henry's side, "developing both the batter for the seafood and the famous tartar sauce. In addition, he hand-canned the pickled beets served at every table. Dressings, coleslaw, sauce and other delicacies were served, to include his homemade lemon pie—available on Sundays."

Next door in 1940, Henry's son, Lambert, managed his dad's fish market. The separate Standard Fish Market sold walleyed pike for eighteen cents per pound and delicious smoked carp for fifteen cents with a call to the original 1930s telephone number of 5002. Offered by Lambert in 1944 were lobster tails, shrimp, oysters, pike, bullhead, sheepshead, carp and suckers. Vincent moved from the Hot Fish Shop to employment at Peerless Chain by 1941, but he returned to join many family members and relatives over the years, serving part time in the kitchen.

The Hot Fish Shop was a quality restaurant enjoyed by travelers and locals. With Blanche Hunter's Tourist Cabins nearly across the street on the "Mankato Dike" in the early years, there was a perfect overnight stopping-off place for Chicago and Minneapolis citizens, as well as occasional outlaws. It was smaller yet similar to the compatriot Oaks Night Club (1931) at Minnesota City—good food, liquor, full-scale orchestras (or pianist) and hosts of people from near and far were there for Saturday night "doings." Like the Oaks, the Hot Fish Shop was a major social center, with talented local musicians and groups as steady fare for weekend diners and dancers in later years.

In the modern era of the 1940s and '50s, very successful people in luxury vehicles from Chicago and all over came to Winona. In earliest days, Henry attempted to make the people even more comfortable. The inclusion of three slot machines (illegal) in the facility in 1935 may have entertained but found Mrs. Henry being charged instead of Henry. She was given a suspended sentence and paid a $100 fine.

Henry was kind to employees over all the years, with well-known Christmas bonuses for all employees—an envied Winona tradition. To celebrate small occasions with employees, he was known to keep a bottle or two on the premises. Unfortunately, raids by liquor agents of 1948 and 1949 found the liquor possession to be interpreted differently. Henry was convicted of the sale of liquor without a license both times.

Henry would suggest that the key to success was family, consistent employees and dedication to food quality. He employed many relatives. In 1955, the year it was named an "Outstanding Café" by the national *McCall's* magazine, he observed, "We don't change personnel. Temperature is very important in preparation of the batter-fried pike....My biggest asset is a knowledge of fish production and marketing and knowing everyone in the field. Commercial fishermen know I know good fish, and they wouldn't think of shipping something inferior to me. They'd get it right back. I can pick my fish."

An interview with a senior former Winonan who enjoyed Tuesday evening dinners at the Hot Fish Shop with his parents called it "a special place to go to. It was special to get a child-sized shrimp cocktail, the personal attention of waitresses and enjoy delicious, batter-fried pike." As he cruises down the hill from Wilson and into town from Interstate 90 when visiting these days, he misses seeing "the landmark" of Winona.

The sponsorship of bowling teams and youth sports teams kept the Standard Fish/Hot Fish Shop name before the public for many years. "Potato Chips and Fish Market Win" announced the Class D bowling results. Since the beginning, Standard Fish sponsored a bowling team that did exceptionally well. Vince and L.J. were on the team of 1933 before the competition heated up. L.J. had a 200 game, with both having mediocre averages.

Competition between the Peerless Chain "Potato Chips" and the "Fish Folks" was fierce for years at the Winona Athletic Club on Mankato Avenue—all right in the heart of St. Stan's Church and the Polish National Alliance, each counting Kowalewskis as members. The leader of the bowling family was Lambert, who rolled a 245 single and 672 errorless in 1944. A skilled athlete, Lambert was also the third baseman for Duluth Dukes, the Lacrosse Blackhawks and the PNA (Winona Chiefs) from 1938 to the mid-'50s.

The very best bowlers of the time rolled for the Standard Fish/Hot Fish Shop team over the years, including local sensations Gordy Fakler (683) and Jerry Dureske (709) of the 1960s. With averages of 187 to 193 in 1960, the "dynamic duo" of Fish Shop bowlers were named four of the top five bowlers of the year in Winona (each bowling in two leagues).

A long-range bowler who stayed with Gordy, Jerry and the team for several years was Dick Schultz, originally from Dakota. He passed through LaCrosse and Dakota by train on his weekly five-hundred-mile round trip from Milwaukee to Winona, arriving just in time for the 7:00 p.m. roll-off. He slept on the train.

Lambert, appointed to the park board in 1949, was pictured in 1966 at Lake Winona with lifetime commercial fisherman and friend Bud Ramer stocking the lake with northern pike. Lambert offered that he was "interested in restoring fishing in the lake for the kids." Lambert also led the charge for lake aeration and the removal of thousands of pounds of rough fish.

In addition to pulling nets of fish off the Mississippi winter and summer, his friend found time, like Lambert, to soak a line. Bud won the biweekly contest at Jackson's Bar on Mankato Avenue with a one-pound, twelve-ounce crappie. Fittingly, the prize was a thirty-six-bottle case of L'il Bub's Beer.

Lambert stayed in the kitchen as his father had done and supported the kids of the community. Each summer at the bandshell, hundreds of Winona kids assembled for Hobo Days. A little-known secret is that the Hot Fish Shop donated the thirty-gallon containers of mulligan stew. All the little hobos and queens delight yet today in remembrance of the epicurean gifts of Henry, Lambert and Mose.

Lambert ventured out of the kitchen on many occasions to greet guests at the front door on Mankato Avenue in his T-shirt, white apron

Lambert Kowalewski carried on the traditions of the Hot Fish Shop for many years as owner and hardy greeter. *Courtesy Winona History Center.*

and smoking a cigar. With a loud "Come on in!" you knew you were in a place of welcome. Pickled beets and Bub's Beer were on the table.

Winona Chiefs manager Emil Scheid brought "Moose" Skowron of the New York Yankees for a cold beer and pike lunch in 1954. Donald Duck's voice made it in 1962 for an extemporaneous performance at the Hot Fish Shop in the form of Clarence Nash, Walt Disney's character voice of Donald for twenty-eight years. Clarence was a shirttail relative of Henry's through marriage. In minutes, Clarence "had the place in a riot." Barry Goldwater didn't get there for his campaign of 1964, but he sent his agent Wendell Corey, noted television actor of the times, for lunch with other notables.

Henry died in 1966 at age seventy-seven, succeeded by his only son, Lambert. Henry had "always cherished good friends, good food and good fishing and he achieved a plentiful supply of all three. What came first, his love of fishing or his love of eating what he caught, he won't even discuss," according to Lambert in the *Republican-Herald*.

He also adored his roots in Poland and asked Lambert "as a dying wish" to visit Poland for him. The Kasubian area of Poland has many Winonans sharing roots there. It resembles the Winona area, with lakes and rivers and fishing. Lambert in 1974 brought home with him the well wishes of the Polish people and a set of artworks, crafts and artifacts to enhance the new Fisherman's Lounge.

The Hot Fish Shop added the fifty-six-by-thirty-foot addition between the restaurant and Fish Company to offer "your favorite cocktail." After many years, Lambert secured a liquor license in 1969. With the development of the improved Highway 14/61 in 1954, Henry and Lambert purchased an additional .76 acre on the corner for the Hot Fish Shop and participated in the additional purchase of 7.8 acres by Winona Hotels.

As a condition of receiving the liquor license, Lambert had to divest himself of interest in the Winona Hotels property and Linahan's Holiday Inn across the roadway, since he could not be a part of two liquor licenses.

The Hot Fish Shop attempted to duplicate its presence with restaurants in Rochester and Mendota Heights over the years. Success was marginal, and those facilities closed after a several-year effort in the 1970s. The absence of Henry and Lambert and Mose, concern over "high overhead" and a series of factors caused the Hot Fish Shop to end its reign "in the shadow of Sugar Loaf" in 1999. The property was sold to Winona Excavating in 2000, with a current Dairy Queen built on the hallowed fish grounds the following year.

An attempt was made in September 2011 by a grandson-in-law with original recipes for batter and sauces to "return to the restaurant's roots." He re-created a Hot Fish Shop in a small center in Rochester, offering batter-fried pike and a variety of options to a new set of customers and allowing the pickled beets and frog legs of the past to continue in Henry and Mose's tradition. At last word, the owner was hoping for a beer license to add the hometown flavor and setting of Bub's Beer and Sugar Loaf to his new space.

Pepin Pickles and Relishes

Zest to Your Picnic Lunch

Polly, Polly, why the pickle?
Eating pickles all the day?
Faith! To make my cheeks more rosy
For my laddie far away.

—*Pepin Pickle ad, March 1927*

A leisurely drive north on two-lane Wisconsin Highway 35 from Winona takes one along the beautiful Mississippi River. Passing farmsteads, we pass through Fountain City, Alma, Nelson, Diamond Bluff and Maiden Rock and glide into Pepin, birthplace of water skiing and Laura Ingalls Wilder's *Little House on the Prairie* setting. (She also lived there.)

Ralph Samuelson actually tied his wood slats and clothesline to the back end of his powerboat across Lake Pepin in 1922 at Lake City. Yet he invented water skiing by circling the lake on his slats to pass by the dock in front of the old pickle factory of Pepin, just off Prairie Street. It isn't known whether Laura had stopped by on the momentous day.

Sitting on today's deck at the Pickle Factory Restaurant of Pepin, we can imagine Ralph pulling up for a beer and brat, to be covered with homemade Pepin Pickle Sauerkraut and mustard, accompanied by a zesty, tart Pepin Pickle.

Although Romans, Chinese and the people of India were creating earlier versions of sauerkraut more than four thousand years ago, including the salting and pickling of cabbage and turnips, the "good stuff" was being created by the Pepin Brand Pickle Company. Originated and incorporated in 1904 in Pepin, Wisconsin, by E.S. LaFrance, the Pepin factory was moved shortly thereafter to Winona.

In June 1917, to gain greater manufacturing capacity and soon-to-be worldwide distribution of pickles, sauerkraut, relishes and the like, LaFrance located at 602 East Front Street in Winona, the former riverside site of the massive Empire Lumber Company.

While the 90-by-168-foot two-story building with basement was being constructed, he headquartered at Lafayette and Front with Western Coal and Ice. He immediately established greater acreage for planting of crops from his original thirty-five acres at Pepin to five hundred in the Winona area—with hopes of one thousand.

He was to purchase from area farmers "cucumbers, cauliflower, cabbage, dill, onions, beans and tomatoes." To service the farmers, he established branch "salting stations" at Lewiston, Pepin, Kellogg and Plainview, soon to add Cochrane, Arcadia and Rushford. By 1925, Pepin had eighteen stations, seven near Winona and eleven in northern Wisconsin, with Rice Lake as the central, northern office.

A salting station takes in cucumbers from the farm. They are weighed, graded, sorted (small for sweet and large for dill), salted and rolled outside in barrels to cure in brine—drained off and refreshed daily. At Lewiston, the largest of stations with 110 acres feeding it in 1915, more than 2 million pickles were sorted.

The barrels were then shipped to the factory, where the one-year pickling and canning processes occurred. Similarly, "excellent" cabbage by the carload from Stockton, Plainview and Kellogg was processed into sauerkraut at the factory in one-hundred-bushel vats. With thirty people employed at the factory, sixteen varieties of products were being processed, canned, bottled and shipped to war and to eight states.

Products advertised in 1928 by Pepin Pickling ("A Winona Institution") were olives; sweet, sour and dill pickles; chow-chow; pearl onions; mustards; horseradish; and sauerkraut. Its "New Product" of the day was sauerkraut juice. ("Try a can tomorrow!")

LaFrance reported that he was "well pleased with business done" and "the output of the Winona plant is in high demand." In 1918, he sought and received a new (lower) pickle shipping rate (for pickles and sauerkraut) from the railroad rate commission and the St. Paul and Great Western Railroad. The year 1919 showed a "large guaranteed government wheat price" that diminished available cucumber acres. Yet LaFrance persevered

The Pepin Pickle Factory of 602 East Front Street, Winona, originated in Pepin, Wisconin, in 1904. Photo 1920s. *Courtesy Winona History Center.*

and prospered. In 1919, farmers were paid an average of $446.66 per acre for their cucumbers.

He had gained his one thousand acres. Along the way, Pepin was assisted by Napoleon, who played a big part in pickle history. Napoleon had promoted pickles as a way to help feed his troops on the march. World War I generals felt the same, knowing that canned pickles and sauerkraut from Pepin were "a very necessary part of a well-balanced ration for a soldier." With "products in demand and distributed to all parts of the U.S.," E.S. LaFrance announced in 1921 the doubling of his plant, as "business has doubled since 1917, with 100,000 bushels of cucumbers handled."

As a Pepin Pickle ad read in 1927:

> *HEALTH AND BEAUTY IN PICKLES*
> *The natural appetite of boys and girls tells the story. Pickles are a natural appetizer, a natural intestine cleanser of the digestive tract and of the bloodstream as well.*

For beauty also, there is something to say for the virtue of the pickle. The farther south you go the more popular the sour pickles seem to be. This is the natural craving for the cooling and health action of the acid.

By 1921, Eugene (E.S.) had also become mayor of Winona. He excelled in setting a tone for factory, employees and community. The thrice-elected president of the National Pickle Packers Association of the late '20s and early '30s, he was also a quiet leader on the homefront, creating a city park at the waterfront for citizens along the beautiful levee area of east Winona.

Employees and associates (including son Leo) were a strong presence in the bowling leagues of Winona for more than thirty years. Following the Pepin ad for sauerkraut in 1923, they represented well the company slogan, "You've Tried the Rest—Now Eat the Best!" as first-place finishers in the local rolloff. Joining the venerable St. Paul tourney in 1939 were bowlers Louis Wera, Leo Curran, John Grams, Francis Hamernik and Leo LaFrance. They were the "First-Place Picklers."

Officers of the company in 1931 included E.S. (Eugene), president; C.D. Tearse, vice-president; Leo LaFrance, secretary; and H.J. McConnon, treasurer. They led the company to success and to "twenty-five consecutive

Tables shown overlook the Mississippi River at Lake City, Minnesota, for a Wisconsin view. *Author's collection.*

years of dividends." E.S. died in April 1951 at age eighty, having put fifty years of leadership into pickles and the greater community. Succeeded by Leo, he managed the company for several years and ultimately sold it in 1956 to the Squire Dingee Company.

By 1958, the Winona company had closed, to be incorporated in Chicago with the Ma Brown brand of pickles and the jams of Squire Dingee. Leo—a most involved community leader in Elks, Boy Scouts, Legion, Rotary and a host of other groups and activities—left the pickle business to run for the state legislature in 1958 while in his new position at Lake Center Switch. His lifetime residence at 409 West Wabasha was within a block of his father's residence. Together they had created a great run in pickles and sharing.

Ma Brown was sold to Beatrice foods in the 1980s. Con Agra of Omaha assumed Beatrice and today owns any vestige of the Pepin Pickle Brand within its huge food stable, alongside Orville Redenbacher, Dannon Yogurt, Hebrew National and a hundred others.

Leo died in 1967 at age seventy-one. He would advise us (as stated in a Pepin ad of 1921) that Pepin pickles and sauerkraut "are an excellent winter and spring tonic for the appetite." He suggested we should all "Try a meal of Pepin Sour Kraut once a week, at least."

The Winona Chiefs

A History of Semipro Baseball in Winona

Summer adventure for boys in our small town of the 1950s revolved around home and neighborhood. We had chores to do, freedom to wander, playground activities, bike hikes, ball games, BB guns and supper at six. Without permission, if chores were done, we could head out to the hills for a campout, zip off to the playground on a makeshift bike for games or quickly organize a bike hike to the country and neighboring small towns with a supply of peanut butter sandwiches and Ritz crackers in a bike basket.

An evening at the local park as fans of our hometown semiprofessional baseball team, the Chiefs, was the highlight of any week. On bikes as a quasi-gang or sitting on freshly cleaned milk cans in the darkened back end of Mr. Valentine's milk hauling truck, we arrived fired up to see our heroes.

Locals "Big George" Vondrashek, Chet Wieczorek, Lambert Kowalewski, All-American Paul Giel and Norm Snyder had their chance at the majors and initially or ultimately (after time in the majors) played with the Chiefs. These were guys from Winona, Rollingstone, Arcadia, Pepin or other little burgs around the Hiawatha Valley. We had seen most of them at Sunday afternoon pickup games at the "West End Rec" Field—the initial home of the Winona Braves—as they took the steppingstone to the Chiefs lineup.

We watched competing players Bill "Moose" Skowron and Johnny Blanchard before they hit the New York Yankees. Johnny Van Cuyk of the Rochester team and Little Chute, Wisconsin, joined the Brooklyn Dodgers in 1947 with Jackie Robinson. Other players were either "going up" to the AAA team or "coming down" from their experiences in the major leagues.

Lambert Kowalewski, local all-star for the Winona Chiefs, Duluth Dukes and LaCrosse Blackhawks. *Courtesy Winona History Center.*

Van Cuyk, for example, played in two World Series and then stayed with the Rochester Royals after his time in the majors to live out his life nearby.

We were pleased to watch them pass through as members of visiting teams from Albert Lea, Austin, Rochester, Waseca or other small cities of the Southern Minny League. There was Haake Mehli of Faribault and Sam "Sad Sam," "Red," "Toothpick" Jones, one of the first African American players seen in Winona (by way of the Rochester Royals) and the first to pitch a no-hitter in Major League Baseball, for the Chicago Cubs. Our special import to the hometown Chiefs was Hugh Orphan of Fort Wayne, Indiana (a "submarine ball" pitcher).

These were evenings to remember. Thousands of local townspeople and neighboring farmers crowded into Gabrych Park, a high-ceilinged structure built on gifted land in memory of a war hero from the East End neighborhood. It was a monument to the ambition and dedication of Polish Americans who had settled on their forty-foot "shotgun" lots in the 1870s, not far from the Mississippi River and the logging industry that brought them here. Along with their immense and marvelous St. Stanislaus Polish Catholic Church a few blocks away, this field of dreams was a major source of pride to all.

They were sawyers, hostlers, roustabouts and mechanics who built the industry and the town. If not employed by one of the lumberyards that lined the river, they were locomotive mechanics or members of the line crew for the many railroads of the area.

In 1876, they organized their first baseball team, the Clippers, to win the state tournament. One of the East Enders, Julian Wera, the "Winona Flash," left his meat-cutting job at the Interstate Packing Plant in 1927 to play 38 games at third base for the New York Yankees as they went on to win 110 games and to wallop the Pirates in four games of the World Series. To play alongside Lou Gehrig and Babe Ruth!

Somewhere near the end of the 1940s, the PNA (Polish National Alliance) team that was competing in the Southern Minnesota League changed from an East End model to a more global "Chiefs" brand and proceeded to fill the stands to capacity. On a first-come, first-seated basis, more than two thousand fans arrived at the stands with intent to get one of the prime seats behind home plate.

There were many protected seats in the tall, thirty-row-deep wood-framed enclosure between first and third bases. With a roof overhead and a chicken wire screen in front, early patrons enjoyed protection from the summer rains and the foul balls that didn't sail over the grandstand to *clunk* into a parked car.

The bleachers on the first and third base lines were also good places to be. Although not covered, there was usually action in the bullpen on either side of the field away from the grandstand view. The Chiefs were in the first base dugout, and their bullpen was just beyond. We often liked to be on the third base side to scope out visiting pitchers or make smart comments through the wire to them, as if they couldn't get to us if they wanted!

The third base side also drew more foul balls to keep our attention—nothing like a zinger at your head when you were turned away from the game. Whether caught or bounced off a head, the balls were returned to the team. We could turn them in to the concession stand for a nickel's credit. Those in the stands had to crane their necks to get a look at what we saw up close and personal.

With a home and away schedule to play, there was at least one game at home each week, sometimes two. Observing the tremendous popularity of baseball, town fathers needed to build a second set of bleachers in deep center field to house the hordes.

Every game, home and away, was broadcast live on our local radio station, KWNO. When the Chiefs were away, we gathered around the stand-up radio in the front room to hear the exploits of our heroes broadcast from afar through the inveterate, enthusiastic commentary of Chuck Williams, a local folk hero in his own right. Chuck graduated from St. Mary's College and dedicated his life to Winona radio and local sports.

The Chiefs were our superstars and heroes of summer. They related to baseball-minded young boys, to wide-eyed local girls of all ages and to fathers and family members who plunked down the thirty-five-cent admission. A night at the ballpark was an escape from day jobs in the factories and processing plants with their repetitive tasks. Some slugged cattle or hogs all day in the packing plant, while others watched the continuous welds of links of chain pass by their station in the excessive warmth of the riverside Peerless Chain Factory.

Games took some away from their warm frame houses for a cool summer evening in the open air. Farmers completed evening milking chores early and took a break from fields and chores that would again engage them at 5:00 a.m. the next morning and every morning thereafter. At the home ballpark, with a nickel bottle of Coke and a high fastball coming, all was right on a summer's eve. On special occasions, the Winona Municipal Band played a pregame concert.

The senses were keen for the sound of the collision of a fastball and the Louisville Slugger held in the hands of Norm, our clean-up batter, or a quick, choppy grounder hit by Gabby Hormann, our country-singing, ever-dangerous catcher, who often placed his grounders between the first and second basemen. Gabby composed and recorded "Moon Over Sugar Loaf" while in Winona but went on to fame as Nashville singer Webb Foley.

Each event was a game of excitement and entertainment. It was real life unfolding before us. Real people with names like Gabby or Stan or Norm made it happen. Tomorrow we could see them at their jobs in the stores and factories or just walking down the street. Tonight they were our heroes in woolen white uniforms not unlike those of the New York Yankees pictured in the pages of *Sport* magazine.

Even their foul balls were exciting when hit up and over the multi-layered forest-green, painted grandstand. Flying high over the wood-beamed uprights and tar-papered roof into the star-filled sky, the errant ball more than likely landed with a *thud* on the hood or top of a patron's parked car. A long and fair fly ball headed toward the 350-foot sign brought everyone to their feet. A double play from third to shortstop to first base was a sight and sound to behold.

With an occasional standing ovation, there were cheers enough to shake the rooftops. Wild cheering ensued every night the Chiefs were in town. Games were won and games were lost, but the cheers continued either way. They could do no wrong.

These heroes of summer were heroes to us all. They were heroes who caused us to see ourselves, our potentials. They caused us to dream the dream. Players embodied the effort, the hope and the dreams that the people in our small midwestern town held for them. The war was over and the Great Depression not so very far behind. People were remembering and thankful for the bounty in their lives.

With battles over, most of the boys home and the economy on a constant upswing, there was hope for jobs and a reason for joy, with an eye fixed on a safe and prosperous future. There was again time for celebration in continued and small ways—a church picnic, a night at the ballpark, a walk by the river levee or fishing at lakefront with special friends and a "picnic" of beer on the table. It was enough. Who could ask for any more?

As the evening paper was delivered, as people came home from work, as front porches filled with family and friends to enjoy the cool at the end of the day or as we turned the colored dial on the radio to *Fibber McGee and Molly* or *The Inner Sanctum*, parents, idling visitors and young listeners offered constant recap and rehash of our heroes' exploits on the baseball diamond. The Chiefs' game and the players who made the news were on our daily menu of conversation and anticipation.

With every train from Chicago to Minneapolis or Minneapolis to Chicago going by our front door, we seemed to have new arrivals for the team from Indianapolis or Chicago or points east arriving on a weekly basis. Each new member of the team dazzled us with his hitting or fielding prowess, but each also fanned the flames of our perpetual hero worship. As ballplayers in our small town who might have been small-town boys themselves, there was no doubt that they were "big time" in our eyes.

They weren't any bigger than the local iceman or the high school athletic star or the strapping farmer from across the bridge, but they were larger than life to everyone they met. They had traveled the country. They had experiences of which we could only dream. They were our connection to the future.

One of our favorites was Emil, a little bit of a guy who played shortstop. He probably didn't weigh more than one hundred pounds. In the long shadows of late afternoon and early evening at the ballpark, his five-foot-two frame took on dimensions that were as long as the shadows cast. He was then as big as his actions. He was the playmaker of the team who fired everyone up, the "chatterbox" throughout nine innings who encouraged the pitcher, batters and his fellow fielders; he set the tone for the hundreds and sometimes thousands of fans.

We didn't need a speaker system to hear Emil. He was perpetually in celebration of the joy of living and his love for the game. Quick playmaking, double-play gyrations and positive spirit were his trademarks. When you met him on the street, he was whistling.

He had come from tryouts in the Chicago White Sox network and World War II army baseball on Guadalcanal (although he was in the navy) to find a home with us. Even though pursued by other teams, he chose to stay and become a backbone of the team and a mainstay in the town. He played several years against and with the greats of the 1940s.

When other Chiefs like Norm Snyder and Stan Shargey hit the long ball, it was Emil who finessed his way into our hearts with his dips and saves and words of encouragement. At shortstop, he was a formidable challenge to the power of those who stepped to the plate.

From experience and reputation, opposing players knew that any ball hit within twenty-five feet of Emil was a costly out. Taking up the space of a moving billboard, he jumped, leaped and dove for seemingly uncatchable line drives and "too-hot" grounders. A quick flip of the ball to first base and the visitor's batting average was further diminished.

He was the leader, a David on a diamond filled with Goliaths. He knew how to play the ball as well as the crowd. The momentum of the game

Emil Nascak batting at Winona's Gabrych Park, with a typical crowd in the stands. *Courtesy Winona History Center.*

could shift from one of sullen silence and a four-to-two fall-behind score to a stirring moment of hope when Emil performed. As leadoff batter, Emil ignited a spark with a tap from his bat.

More than once, his blooper hit to short center, the stolen base that followed and the long ball of Shargey or Norm placed him in scoring position at third. Hope was alive. A home run would send the devoted into ecstasy. From a near loss to a turnaround, Emil had again led the charge.

Emil's day job was at the Neville's Clothing Store (later St. Clair's), a local haberdashery for the well-to-do and those who wished to be. As years went on, I worked for a while side by side with Emil, selling men's suits and clothing. In no way could I compete. He was the star of the show and the ultimate salesman and playmaker, greeting every customer with warmth, charm and recognition. What a guy! He could sell you a suit and all the trimmings and make you feel like you were the most important man in town.

He would tie together a new suit with the "specials"—the new Arrow shirt, tie, belt and socks to match. The top-quality suits of Hart, Shaffner and Marx were Emil's specialty, finished off with a Harris Tweed topcoat. It was top quality in a quality-conscious America after the war, all served up by the greatest ballplayer in town. Who could ask for anything more?

When one came to town to be fitted by a master like Emil, the new suit owner felt "like a million bucks," as Emil was wont to say. Having met Emil in the process was a special bonus, at least equal to having a signed baseball card of Phil Rizzuto or Warren Spahn.

While Emil was selling suits, his longtime compatriot in the infield, Stan Shargey, was hard at work at the Badger Machine Company on West Fifth Street. He was doing his part to create the newly patented HOPTO digger to be sold around the world for construction jobs—later under the Warner-Swasey brand.

A real bull-nose at third and at work, Stan stood five-foot-nine and weighed in at 180 pounds—all muscle and power. His shot from third burned the hand of the first baseman.

He was serious and deliberate and knew his way around both third base and around manufacturing, having previously served on an army baseball team during the war and as a baseball team member and employee of the General Electric Voltmen of Fort Wayne, Indiana, the national semipro champions. In between times, he played AAA ball at Sacramento and Oklahoma City and the Rome Colonels. His teammate was Hugh Orphan, the Chiefs' manager.

Luck and friendship must have drawn Hugh, Stan, Emil and others to Winona. Many found the home they sought, for they gave up the wanderlust of pro ball and settled in for a lifetime of steady citizenry in Winona. I knew Stan at Warner-Swasey and found him to be a hardworking, fun-loving type of guy with a ready smile and a story a day that I could carry on to the next manufacturing spot on my vending route.

Hugh was a successful upholsterer in town for many years with his shop on East Broadway. When visiting my mother-in-law in 2000 at the Lake Winona Manor, I looked in on him shortly before his death. I told him of my Chiefs memories.

Hugh started with the Wausau Timberjacks in 1940, winning twenty games each for a few years. He completed his professional circuit in 1948 as a member of the AAA Sacramento Sunbeam Bread, where his record was less stellar. He still had it in the 1950s with the Chiefs, a red-hot fastball that came at you nearly underhanded.

Our parents were terrific, but ball playing was a kids' game. They walked their walk of hard work and the Protestant work ethic. Limits of hard work,

The Southern Minny All-Star team of 1952 included Winona Chiefs. *Lower row, left to right*: Emil Nascak; Bill Leach; Dick Czaplewski; no. 4 unknown; no. 5 Jerry Wineski; nos. 6, 7 and 8 unknown; and no. 9 Hugh Orphan, Chiefs manager/pitcher. *Top row, left to right*: no.1 unknown; no. 2 Paul Giel; no. 3 Eddie Gittens; no. 4 Butch Wieczorek; no. 5 George VonDrashek; and nos. 6, 7, 8 and 9 unknown. *Courtesy Winona History Center.*

church and heritage tended to remove fun from their lives. Their lives had begun with chores on the farm when they were four years of age and continued on a fast-forward march of work and doing from that day on.

They didn't seem opposed to our having fun with the games of baseball, kick the can or hide-and-seek. It seemed that they just hadn't had the experience. In their quiet ways, they remained good observers and supporters of our actions and those of our real-life heroes, the Chiefs. They didn't put down our dreams and comments and moments of excitement.

It is so interesting to discover that Pa, in his time as a junior high youth of German-Lutheran heritage, was named one of the most outstanding athletes in the early part of the twentieth century on the playlot in the east end of town. There were about 1,800 kids who participated, yet the newspaper story I discovered in the archives named my Pa and our neighbor, Carl, as the two most promising of all. To my knowledge, Pa never attended a Chiefs game. I never knew that we shared the talk or walked the walk.

We were a fortunate few to be fans of the 1950s. Baseball was fun. Pitches and catches in the big games of the Chiefs zip into our memories. Even the fish-fly invasion that covered the night and caused game lights at our riverside park to be shut off for a bit to dissuade the creatures was an event.

Having heroes of the Chiefs' hardball in our midst was a treasure. We learned about curve balls and bonks on the head. Even more, memories of a comfortable childhood of work and play linger. We learned that dreams are achievable. We learned that life is meant to be good.

Strikeouts, Athleticism and Guts

THE PAUL GIEL STORY

He was from just down the street. As a ten-year-old watching him on the baseball and football field or the basketball court, I knew that I wanted to be like him. "The best high school pitcher in Minnesota sent sixteen Rochester batters down as he issued only two walks—to claim the Big Nine High School Title." He had beaten Red Wing 3-0 in the morning with a no-hit, no-run game. In thirteen innings of pitching that day, Paulie struck out twenty-eight batters and gave up only four hits.

All this from a guy who tossed his tennis ball at the back of his small house on Sioux Street and at the brick-walled back of our shared Madison School, where I tried to similarly imprint my pitches on the wall a few years later. He was a genuine gum-chewing sidewalk walker of the neighborhood whom thousands would scream for on WCCO radio broadcasts from the U of M's Memorial Stadium on sparkling Saturday afternoons of autumn in the early '50s.

Like the rest of us over the years, Paul Giel had twirled the Tilt-a-Whirl at Steamboat Days, skated at the Athletic or Lakeside rink in winter and worked a part-time job to help with personal finances. "Paulie" was everywhere, from leading the "Federal Breads" to victory at age fourteen in the Midget Baseball League to scoring buckets on Saturday mornings at Washington-Kosciusko School to set a new scoring record of 1946. With his buddy Noel Holst gaining eleven of the winning twenty-four points, Paul played "a good defensive game" to help win the eighth-grade match for Central against cross-town rival Jefferson. Even when he didn't score, he was featured. By

1949, at Winona High School, Giel had passed the pigskin forty-five yards to Holst, who "went in standing up" to beat Northfield. The boys were also co-captains of the basketball team the same year.

Paul first showed up in the newspaper in 1942, when at age ten he helped win two games for the Blackhawks of the Midget League, with two singles in two separate games. He was also the pitcher of one game, winning 19–3. With brother Alden, Paul at age ten joined the West End Midget All-Stars to beat the East Enders 17–9. With brother Ed, the Giels (Paul and Ed) gained six hits, including a homer in a game of 1942. They went on to the double header for Midget All-Stars at Rochester.

We crossed the same paths. From the YMCA or the "Vars," we walked Huff Street toward McVey's Ice Cream Shoppe for a nickel pumpkin or "zebra" ice cream cone, shared the same teachers at Madison School and saw Mrs. Thorn and her dog, Max, of Thorn's Grocery at Howard and Dacota Streets on a near-daily routine.

We played on the same dangerous railroad tracks crossing through town, avoiding twenty or more trains passing through day and night. In the Giels' small "shotgun" house nearly touching the sidewalk only one hundred yards away from the tracks, Paulie heard (and felt) the steady rumble and *click-clack* of wheels, locomotives and boxcars. His father, Ed, went off each week to drive these same monsters for the Chicago and Northwestern Railroad. Mrs. Giel worked hard at Jones & Kroeger, played the piano at the Elks and coordinated PTA activities at Madison School where Paul, brothers and sister attended.

A neighbor boy of the time remembered that Paul's father, Edward, was an engineer for the Chicago and NW Railroad, needing to be gone on his travels over the weeks. With the same train track but a football field away from Paul's bedroom, Paul heard the thunder of the engines and knew that his father was working. Mother Marion was also at work. With the four Giel kids, the Wessin kids across the street, Doug and others, there was a band of neighbor kids streaming around and through the neighborhood at will. According to ninety-three-year-old Doug of today, it was a scene of "Katy, bar the door!"

I could already sense the greatness as I delivered the daily paper to the home of Edward of Indiana (German) and Marion of Minnesota (Irish) on Sioux Street. At 520 Sioux, Marion played her piano and orchestrated the family in a small house not unlike so many of the houses inhabited by early laborers of Winona's lumber, chain making and meatpacking industries. Her parents lived practically next door.

On opening day of 1946, Giel pitched a one-hitter with ten strikeouts.

A little more than a week later, on June 13, he struck out twenty-one batters in a seven-inning game. The following month he only got better, pitching a no-hitter for the Federal Bread team versus the Merchant Banks team, with 19 strikeouts in seven innings. For Federal Bread he had 252 outs in 1946, with an astounding 223 being strikeouts! He also led the league in hitting.

In 1948 and 1949, when he was still in high school, Giel played shortstop for the Rollingstone team of the Bi-State League (a Minnesota amateur league).

Giel overpowered his competition with his fastball, and national scouts like Angelo "Tony" Giuliani were starting to take notice of his dominance.

There's something about a hometown hero. When you saw one on the sidewalk or watched one at the high school football or basketball game, you knew that there was hope for you. Someone showed the way. I remember Tom Kane of the high school basketball team who walked by in sixth grade when I held my patrol boy flag on Broadway. And he smiled.

Ben Lee of Cotter basketball and Jerry Palbicki of west end baseball fame, along with all the other powerful athletes of the East End who often attended the Catholic high school, became strong models. Quarterback Bill Morse of the Winona Winhawks and Mill Street visited our street-side touch football games, along with Jim Klahr of Winona State.

As a skinny 112-pound wrestler in seventh grade, I saw Jim Blake, Moose Erickson and the DeLozier brothers wrestle. Jerry Ziebell and Jerry, Stuart and Morrie Miller swam for glory. The heroes were everywhere. The stars were aligned in Winona year after year, as they are today. Young men and women continually set new standards in athletics for the younger ones.

I saw Paul Giel and Noel Holst up close and personal and watched with awe the skills of "H-Bomb" Heise, whose jump shot was pictured in the center of an H-Bomb blast in the local paper. Tenold Milbrandt jumped and amazed and made it to All-State basketball forward. And I had to guard him as a fledgling sophomore!

Jefferson Field and School hosted Friday night football games (in the space now known as Paul Giel Field) and postgame "sock hops." The West End "Rec" field gave us Max Molock, summer baseball and the Winona Braves. Howie's Varsity Inn a block from the high school was a second home to many, not unlike the "Happy Days" of Fonzie's era. The gleaming maple floors caused by custodian Fred Tarras's efforts on Winona High's basketball court invited us all.

Pictured are 1950s local stars of the Winona High School swim team: Jerry Miller, Bruce Krings, Mike Hull (*above*) and Jerry Ziebell, surrounding Coach Lloyd Luke at the Latsch Beach. *Courtesy Winona History Center.*

"Paulie" led the way. He dominated the Midgets, was the leading scorer in basketball, led the summer American Legion team and was Winona's "Athlete of the Year" in 1949 and 1951. Wearing no. 46 in basketball and no. 7 in football at Winona High, Paul performed for notable Winona coaches Ed Spencer and Gordy Addington—the same coaches the author followed a few years later. Paul lettered in football, baseball, basketball and wrestling and was included on the 1950 Minnesota All-State High School Football Team.

Paul (at 112 pounds) joined brothers Alden (at 133 pounds) and Ed (at 145) to lose in wrestling for Winona High at Austin in 1946. The best effort was Ed's draw, with Alden decisioned and Paul pinned.

Paul beat crosstown Cotter in baseball against rival pitcher Harold "Popeye" Wychgram in 1950. He lost in 1948 to Carl Starzecki yet beat those Ramblers in 1949, 6–4. Popeye, of Cotter and the Winona Hornets Hockey Team, was a teenage superstar in his own right (at goalie) and Cotter baseball fame. Watching these games was to see all the stars of Winona athleticism.

After quarterbacking Eddie Spencer's Winhawks in 1949, Paul and friend Charles "Chuck" Radechal went on to the U of M. Chuck was "all-state" and undefeated as heavyweight wrestler for two years. He was Paul's right tackle and would play along with him for the Gophers. Paul finished his high school basketball career in District 3 playoffs against perennial challenger Rochester Rockets. The Winhawks lost 50–41, but Paul earned 15 of those 41 points.

The only thing Paul didn't do was "rassle" against the pros on Saturday nights at the Redmen's Wigwam, as former University of Minnesota stars Bronko Nagurski and Vern Gagne had done. He did, however, have his name up in lights in 1953 on the marquee of the State Theatre of Winona, where twelve-inch letters stated "South Sea Woman and Paul Giel." Those shimmering lights of Johnson Street could be seen from the Varsity Inn, where Paul and others enjoyed Howie's burgers and nickel Cokes.

He led the Winona Braves (of Athletic Park fame) against Winona's bigger-brother Winona Chiefs and struck out local all-star and Hot Fish Shop owner Lambert Kowalewski and eight others. Paul played a lot of games for the Braves, with Rusty Podjaski as catcher, beating everyone from Alma to Trempealeau, Lewiston and beyond, with a no-hitter in 1950 in which he "fanned 17!"

Along with Emil Nascak of the Winona Chiefs, Paul worked part time at Neville's. By then he was already a record-breaking sophomore at the University of Minnesota. He beat Austin for the Chiefs in 1952 while a student at the U of M. He couldn't get out lead-off batter Ray Gabrych of the Chiefs, however. The Gabrychs were World War II–era baseball all-stars, with the east end home of the PNA/Chiefs named for one of the brothers lost in the war.

Hugh Orphan, Winona Chiefs baseball team manager and "submarine pitcher," said that Paul's "heart and guts make him the great athlete that he is." Paul pitched for the Chiefs in the summer. After a slow spring and Gopher start in 1951, Paul meekly asked pitching star Hugh if he wanted him back on the team. With contract in hand, there was no doubt.

Pitching for the Braves against the Chiefs (with 2,100 Winona fans in attendance, a typical eve at Gabrych Park) and striking out ten in the process, Paul was awarded a Bing Crosby raincoat by the Boland Manufacturing Company of Winona for the feat. Paul's record with the Braves was 5-0 in 1951.

Everywhere you looked, he "fanned nine or fourteen or twenty," even twenty-six in one day! Record-setting coach Dick Siebert of U of M baseball said, "He's the best I've seen." Cohort and nationally known U of M football coach Bernie Bierman said that Giel was "the best halfback he had ever seen at Memorial Stadium" (and only in his freshman year).

It was with great excitement that we all listened to Paul's exploits with the Golden Gophers on WCCO radio in the early '50s. As Frank Litsky of the *New York Times* noted in 2002:

> As a 5-foot-11-inch, 185-pound single-wing tailback for Minnesota from 1951 through 1953, Giel (pronounced GEEL) received an athletic scholarship that covered only tuition, so he worked in a brewery to earn money for room and board. Over three years, he ran and passed for 4,110 yards and 35 touchdowns.
>
> As a senior, he finished a close second to Johnny Lattner, the Notre Dame quarterback, in the voting for the Heisman Trophy as the year's outstanding college player. He was later elected to the National Football Foundation's College Hall of Fame.

Paul led the nation in total yards in 1953. Leaving the Chiefs behind for the summer, he declared as he left for summer ROTC training, "I love baseball as much as I love football." Giel was to be a professional baseball pitcher.

Paul did not choose the golf circuit. When he took it up before leaving for ROTC in 1953, the local pro described him as "a natural," shooting in the low 80s. Paul said that he "shunned the sport during his high school days because he thought it was sissified."

After his collegiate days in baseball, again as All-American, he chose to go to baseball (for a $60,000 bonus) with the New York and San Francisco

Paul Giel celebrates at one of the many banquets held in his honor in Winona and the nation. As one of the best American athletes of all time, he was All-American in baseball and football at the University of Minnesota in the 1950s. *Courtesy Winona History Center.*

Giants and then the Pittsburgh Pirates, Minnesota Twins and Kansas City Athletics. Yogi Berra was seen talking to him for the Yankees at Toot Shor's restaurant in New York.

From 1954 to 1961, with two years off for active duty as an army officer, he earned an overall record of 11-9, mostly as a relief pitcher.

Mother Marion set a strong standard of religion and work and positive expectation, to be rewarded by a kiss in 1953 by Coach Wes Fesler at a Curtis Hotel banquet in Minneapolis honoring Paul. "Ma and Pa" were also feted as a model for families and youth. Paul couldn't have done it "without his good parents and their emphasis on church and school."

Bernie Bierman, august coach of the Gophers, placed Paul at left half in Paul's freshman year. Wes Fesler, the new coach the following year, made him quarterback. After three games, he was "back at left half—and calling the signals and punts."

He was named to the All-Catholic Collegiate Football Team. Becoming captain of the Gopher team in 1953, he was given the symbolic "flaming torch of leadership." He was also named *Look* magazine's Player of the Year.

A few years later, Emil and I carried on men's suit and clothing sales in the same store where Paul had earlier been pictured outfitting his manager, Hugh Orphan. We hoped for "Paulie"—as Emil called him—to stop by.

Don Riley, famed sports columnist, said of the Gopher team, "Nothing has happened to the Minnesota campus in years like [the arrival of] Giel.… Here's a 19-year-old sophomore with the poise and personality of an old pro.…To hear him tell it, his abilities are the result of good fortune experienced in the line of competing…soon to be setting a record superior to any Gopher before him."

Paul Giel, the "North Star," was lauded by Grantland Rice, the nation's premier sportswriter of the times, at a New York dinner at Toots Shore's Restaurant in 1953:

> *Around the ends, or through the line,*
> *Along the ground or in the air,*
> *You set a tingle in the spine.*
> *You travel where the touchdowns fare.*
> *Your flying feet all seem to say—*
> *We're headed for the winning clover—*
> *For we still sing upon our way*
> *"On to the goal again—and over."*
>
> *In raging battle rout and reel.*
> *Skoal to Minnesota's Giel.*
> *And once again another skoal.*
> *The North Star shines in fame and flame.*
> *For those who turn to fight and live*
> *Just add the line—he played the game.*
>
> *He gave the best he had to give.*
> *For others let the welkin ring*
> *High-answered up to the hills of God.*
> *But here tonight we crown him king*
> *Of all whose cleats ripped up the sod.*

Paul Robert Giel was born on February 29, 1932, in Winona, Minnesota. He was married in 1957 to Nancy Davis, living in Minnetonka, Minnesota, a Minneapolis suburb. He died in May 2002 of a heart attack, survived by his wife; sons, Paul Jr. and Thomas; daughter, Gerilynn; and six grandchildren.

From 1972 to 1988, Giel was the University of Minnesota's athletic director. Among the coaches he hired were Lou Holtz in football and

Herb Brooks in hockey. Until his death, he was the chief fundraiser for the Minneapolis Heart Institute.

Paul was inducted into the Minnesota Sports Hall of Fame (one of seventy-two total honorees) alongside University of Minnesota coach Bernie Bierman and other erstwhile athletes and supporters like Calvin Griffin, Rod Carew and Bud Grant. He was inducted into the Winona Senior High School Hall of Fame on May 19, 2002.

The Lakers Come to Town

LET THE GAME BEGIN

Dr. James Naismith, the inventor of basketball, played outside as a boy in Ontario. As boys of the Hiawatha Valley do yet today, he played games of catch and hide-and-seek. He also played a medieval game called "Duck on a Rock." It is a game in which a person guards a large "drake stone" from opposing players who try to knock it down by throwing smaller stones at it—combining "tag" and marksmanship. Placing a somewhat large stone on a larger stone or a stump of a tree, one player stays near the stone to guard it.

The other players throw stones at the "duck" in an attempt to knock it off of the platform. Once it is knocked off, the throwers all rush to retrieve their stones. If a player is tagged before returning to the throwing line with his or her stone, he becomes the guard. The guard cannot tag anyone until he picks up a duck at his feet, nor can he chase anyone until he puts the original duck back on its platform. To play Duck on a Rock most effectively, Naismith soon found out that a soft lobbing shot was far more effective than a straight, hard throw, a thought that later proved essential to his invention of basketball.

In 1891, he was directed by his boss, Dr. Luther Gulick of the YMCA of Springfield, Massachusetts, to create a game for boys in fourteen days that would "make it fair for all players and not too rough." Thinking it through, Naismith hung peach crates at a height on either end of a large room, added a soccer ball instead of rocks and nine players on each team. He continued to refine his methods as the first basketball coach at the University of Kansas from 1898 to 1907. Recent findings suggest that "Duck" was a game of intellectual meaning, strategic balance and skill.

I'm so happy that the "Duck on a Rock" success became a reality for Dr. Naismith, the Minneapolis Lakers and the fans of the Hiawatha Valley. Basketball by local teams like the Winona Winhawks, Cotter Ramblers, Winona State Warriors and St. Mary's Redmen filled winter evenings with sparkle and awe, enhanced by visits of our big-city cousins, the Minneapolis Lakers. We are warmed on the cold nights of basketball season yet today by fond memories of our homegrown superstars and their "bigger brothers."

With the likes of Vern Mikkelsen, Joe Hutton, Whitey Skoog and Bud Grant all from within 150 miles of Minneapolis, the Minneapolis (and now Los Angeles) Lakers of the late 1940s could be known as the "homegrown team."

Their Lakers team took off to shatter NBA records and bring professional basketball to life across the state and the nation. In their first year, future Hall of Famer George Mikan of DePaul University (and the defunct Chicago American Gears) led the locals to the National Basketball Association title.

Coach and team leader John Kundla was even more local, having graduated from Minneapolis Central High School and the University of Minnesota. He first coached at DeLaSalle High School, entered the navy to serve on LSTs in World War II and came back to coach the St. Thomas "Tommies."

He was lured to the infant Lakers in their second season for a salary-doubling $6,000 per year in 1947–48. It was the beginning of today's Los Angeles Lakers (now with sixteen NBA championships). Five of the NBA titles came in the first six years for Kundla, with most of his other years spent in division finals.

Kundla remained coach for the team's eleven-year existence in Minneapolis. The team moved to Los Angeles in 1960, sold by new owner Bob Short. Kundla left future Hall of Famer Elgin Baylor at the airport gate, staying behind to coach his beloved alma mater Minnesota Gophers for nine more years. He was inducted into the Naismith Memorial Basketball Hall of Fame in 1995.

Known today as "Showtime" and the Lakers, it took more than a dozen years after leaving Minnesota for Los Angeles to achieve their first stand-alone NBA Championship. Once again, they were on the cusp, with Kobe Bryant and his 29.5 average points per game.

The Minneapolis Lakers! What a team! And they came to see us in Winona in the late 1940s and early '50s at the wide-open high school auditorium stage and three-sided, self-contained basketball court of the Winhawks. We had our eyes opened. In their exhibitions, we could see real stars up close and personal. We ran home to our own "bangboard" to try their shots. We couldn't do as they did, but we were inspired to keep trying the hook shot. We dribbled a bit, but not quite like Slater Martin, who dribbled through six-foot-ten George Mikan's legs.

George Mikan led the team to six NBA championships in seven years with the shot that made him basketball's greatest scorer—the famous hook shot from the pivot. According to general descriptions online, Mikan invented the hook shot and the shot block. As a consequence, the NCAA and later the NBA adopted the goal tending rule, and in 1951, the NBA widened the foul lane, a decision known as the "Mikan rule." For years thereafter, some of us tried our hook shot from the exact spot on the same circle of the high school floor where George Mikan turned his fancy, with less stellar results.

Once settled in after the whiz-bang exhibition game, we got to watch *Mr. Basketball and Co.*, the Lakers' new 1950 movie. Shown on the big white screen set on the auditorium stage, it was the place where we would enjoy high school pepfests, ball games, concerts, our star Winhawk players and the beautiful homecoming queen candidates. Now we were seeing the Lakers in action on our very stage.

Putting the total show together in 1946 for the Lakers was Max Winter. A graduate of Hamline University on a basketball scholarship, he must have liked the coaching of Joe Hutton Sr. and the skills developed by fellow Piper teammates Vern Mikkelsen and Joey Hutton Jr., who soon joined the team.

A sports entrepreneur in all venues, Winter held sway at the Leamington Hotel. He was an erstwhile basketball fan and an entrepreneur before the word was invented. He knew what he was all about and knew how to get the locals behind him. Sid Hartman, Morris Chalfin and Ben Berger joined Max as owners.

Max ran a restaurant specializing in turkey, the 620 Club—by 1950, he was selling more of it than any other site in the United States. He was known as a mover and a shaker. Max also brought us the Minnesota Vikings, the Minneapolis-based National Football League expansion team that began in the 1961 season.

George Mikan joined the team in 1947–48, visiting Winona for the first time that year. After a previous night in Sheboygan, the mighty Lakers found opposition at the high school from "Harold's Studio," a local pickup team.

It was a challenge for the hometown boys to face Jim Pollard, Slater Martin, Big George and the full cast.

Max had gathered his minions and put them on a bus tour around the state and region. Winonans and others could take a look at these giants in their midst. The team traveled to Sheboygan, Mason City, Winona, LaCrosse, Bismarck, Hibbing, Sioux Falls and all the cities of the Big Nine. They even stopped by Pipestone.

Along the way between visits, Mikan was setting new records in NBA competition—first 30 points, then 40 points (a new record) in a game. In 1949, he held an average of 28.5 points per game. "Mr. Basketball" and his team played an official game in Fargo against the Syracuse Nationals in 1951. The college all-stars challenged the Lakers in Winona in 1951, leaving us behind to play next games in Rochester and Hibbing. At Rochester they drew four thousand fans. George went on to score 61 in a league game in 1952.

By 1953, they were back in town at the new Memorial Hall Gymnasium at Winona State Teachers College. Just before Christmas, the floor of the Warriors was polished and properly "broken in." The newspaper announced, "A Tall Tale Is in Store for Winona and Winona-Area Basketball Fans."

And tall they were—six-foot-nine Clyde Lovellette, six-foot-ten George Mikan, six-foot-seven Vern Mikkelsen, six-foot-five Jim Pollard and six-foot-five Dick Schnittker all came to town with five-foot-ten Slater Martin and the full contingent to play the all-stars from the University of Minnesota, including Bud Grant, formerly of the Lakers.

They played on the same floor where we were to see the Harlem Globetrotters. A sold-out crowd of sixteen thousand had seen the two teams together in a big, nationally publicized matchup in Chicago in 1948. There, the "Globetrotters Whip[ped] Lakers" by a score of 61–59, a semi-miraculous event. And here they were in Winona!

The year 1953 also brought the Four Aces, a popular singing group, to St. Paul for the Lakers–Fort Wayne Pistons game on Saturday, with a similar performance at the Lakers–New York Knicks match on Sunday. We were fortunate to hear some of the Laker games on KWNO, with play-by-play by Dick Enroth of WLOL radio, although we had to spin our own 45rpm records of the Four Aces.

In 1956, the Lakers were back in Winona at Memorial Hall, led by Lovellette, Dick Garmaker and Ed Kalafat. Slater Martin stayed with the team until becoming coach of the St. Louis Hawks in 1957. Other players that headed off to coaching included Pollard, Whitey Skoog, Hutton, Mikkelsen and Mikan.

The late '50s brought hard times for the Lakers, with Mikan becoming general manager. Max Winter left after seven years. The team was losing money and fans in 1957 when owner Ben Berger offered, "I'd say we're just one good forward away from being a title contender."

The infusion of superstar Elgin Baylor into the lineup changed the Lakers, as Berger had hoped. Baylor scored twenty-five points in his debut game. In 1959, they won the Western Division, with the superstar scoring fifty-five in one game. They lost their first-year coach in Los Angeles, to be replaced by Jim Pollard.

Shortly before Baylor's arrival, a 1958 regular game saw the Lakers against the Detroit Pistons in Minneapolis. A preliminary game—most likely a benefit—drew the Rockets of Rollingstone's Holy Trinity School (Winona-area) to the big city to face the private school Benilde team. Led by Steve Hengel with 17 points, the Rockets blasted Benilde 43–35.

In years after leaving Minneapolis, and up to 1965, owner Bob Short staged a game "back home" in Minneapolis to benefit Benilde–St. Margaret's School of St. Louis Park, most often a game between the Lakers and the New York Knickerbockers.

The years since have been good to the Lakers, with Kobe Bryant having led the team in recent years with a 29.5 average per game and a free throw average of 86.5 percent. Kobe and his crew haven't stopped by the high school or WSTC, however. George Mikan led the league in 1949 with an average of 27.8.

In a note of tribute, the former Minnesota Vikings headquarters and training facility in Eden Prairie, Minnesota, was named Winter Park in honor of Max Winter. Bud Grant, initial Laker from Superior, was the Vikings' winningest and most successful coach. NFL Coach of the Year in 1969, he was (and is) held in highest regard by all, including esteemed rival coach Vince Lombardi. Grant was elected to the Canadian Football Hall of Fame in 1983 and the Pro Football Hall of Fame in 1994.

George Mikan is seen as one of the pioneers of professional basketball, redefining it as a game of so-called big men with his prolific rebounding, scoring and shot blocking. His great talent was to shoot over smaller defenders. Along with Coach John Kundla, teammate Vern Mikkelsen and owner Max Winter, he was named to the Minnesota Sports Hall of Fame.

A statue of Mikan shooting his trademark, ambidextrous hook shot has graced the entrance to Target Center in Minneapolis since April 2001—the Timberwolves' home only a few blocks from the Lakers' humble beginnings.

He Paddled His Own Canoe

THE MISSISSIPPI RIVER VALLEY'S GREATEST BENEFACTOR

Leaving Zurich in 1854 for places unknown, twenty-two-year-old John Latsch left parents Casper and Barbara in what is today's top-ranked and wealthiest city of the world—where John chose not "to make a base." He booked passage to America, arriving in New Orleans to set north by boat to St. Louis and continued upriver passage to St. Paul. As he traveled northward, he became more acclimatized to the Mississippi River Valley's beauty—rivaling that of his former Wald, Canton, Lake Zurich region of Switzerland.

With ice forming in the river and winter coming on, his steamer was forced to disengage passengers and freight at the village of Dakota, Minnesota, and head back south—one hundred miles short of his goal. John didn't contact his parents over his "peregrinations" upon arrival.

Instead, he went "to work out with brain and muscle my own future [and] career—industry being one of my inherited virtues," according to the Winona Newspaper Project. He bought an axe and soon found work as a chopper of cordwood and feller of trees. He was well known around Nathan Brown's Dakota Store and appreciated as an intelligent, hardworking young man. His new friend Nathan was "one of Winona County's earliest householders—engaged in the Indian Trade at Dakota."

Soon missed around the store's potbellied stove, John had moved across the river to Wisconsin in 1856 to become a teacher and farmer. John resolved, "Henceforth I shall devote my time and energy to thrift, to create a local habitation, and also for the development of good citizenship in the free

Vegetables grown on John Latsch's Wisconsin farm led him to create a wholesale grocery outlet in Winona, Minnesota, of grand scale, leading to personal success and significant family contributions of public land—more than eighteen thousand acres! *Author's collection.*

republic of my adoption." His "local habitation" was then in the river valley near Centerville, Dodge and Trempealeau, Wisconsin—across and upriver from his landing spot at Dakota.

John's role as Wisconsin farmer lasted until 1864, when he joined his new country's Northern army in the Civil War, serving with General Sherman in his "March to the Sea." After the war, John and Anna, his wife of eight years, settled into life as grocer of Winona, beginning in 1867. He soon joined Mr. Preece to ultimately form with him "one of the Northwest's largest wholesale grocery suppliers—Preece and Latsch Grocery House." Soon thereafter, around January 1875, John was reported to be "packing the space under his sidewalk with ice for summer use." Preece and Latsch lasted until 1892, when the company became "John Latsch and Son."

Anna and John had two sons—John A. and Edward. Sadly, two daughters (Nettie and Emma) died early. Edward left school at sixteen and worked as a billing clerk for his father until his passing in October 1909, the year of his father's death. He had accompanied his father and his father's new wife to Switzerland in 1900. Only days before his death, Edward was moved to a sanitarium in Hudson, Wisconsin. Mother Anna had passed away in 1898, with John remarrying in 1899.

Remaining son John A., Winona's benefactor of thousands of acres of Mississippi River frontage and adjoining properties, was born on August 15, 1860 in Trempealeau County, three miles from Dodge, where father John was a pioneer settler in Latsch Valley.

John A. was elected mayor of the city of Winona in 1905. In addition to his many personal gifts of land, he secured in 1906 a "perpetual lease of part of

Flowers in recognition of the personal losses within the Latsch family. *Author's collection.*

the island [across from Winona] for a public bathing beach from owner CNW Railroad," as noted in the *Republican-Herald*. The following year, a city board was initiated and a bathhouse was built, with John A. providing the necessary $10,000 for building. A rental lease fee of $10 per year was paid to CNW through all the years, although the property was never listed as a taxable entity.

LATSCH, VAN GORDER AND BATHING BEACH FUN

Known initially as Island No. 72 of the Mississippi River, the first settlement of the sand island may be attributed to Captain S.W. VanGorder. VanGorder operated a ferry between the island and Winona from 1865 to 1880. The right-of-way was granted to him by the Chicago Northwestern Railroad Company, successor to the Winona and Southwestern Railroad Company. His first ferry trip was on May 27, 1865.

By 1868, VanGorder "built the first road across the Trempealeau bottoms and induced the Burbank Stage Co. to cross the ferry to Winona." The linkage was probably in line with the newly established mail routes to Eau Claire and St. Paul.

VanGorder's boat, the seventy-foot *Turtle*, could carry four double teams (of horses). The *Turtle* lasted until 1878, when the captain built his ninety-five-foot steamer *VanGorder*, capable of carrying twelve double teams. Rates of crossing (one way) were forty cents for double team (horses), fifteen cents for man and horse and five cents for a foot passenger, with hogs and sheep at two and a half cents each. In 1880, VanGorder left the enterprise, selling boat and business to the city. City staff operated the *VanGorder* from 1880 to 1887, when VanGorder bought back his boat. It later burned on the island.

In an 1881 entry of city council minutes in the *Winona Republican*, it was noted that Captain VanGorder was paid $3.00 for cordwood for the engine house. In the same minutes, Alderman John Latsch's grocery business was paid $20.84 for "goods for ferry and charges for paupers."

In 1883, father John joined other city leaders and contributed "$25.00 to the Rochester Fund" for an apparent cyclonic disaster. Son John was everywhere, as grocer and alderman and city supporter; even recruited as one of the judges at the Baby Show of 1898. The shop at 223 East Third Street invited mothers to bring their babies, with cash prizes for prettiest blonde, fattest girl, smallest boy, sweepstakes prizes (five) and others. After closing time, fifty additional entries were refused.

VanGorder had been entrepreneur, developer and precursor to any bridge across the sloughs and river at Winona. His roadway laid the route and structure through the sloughs and marshes to become base footings for the Winona High Wagon Bridge, opened in 1892. Permission was granted to Winona and Southwestern Railroad by the U.S. War Department to build a railway bridge and structure in 1890. A pontoon bridge was first proposed to replace the ferry, but this was refused. The High Wagon Bridge thus moved ahead, with considerable concern for finding the necessary $100,000 of funds needed to open on

The High Wagon Bridge across the Mississippi from the Latsch Island (1892) terminated at the foot of Main Street in Winona, Minnesota. *Author's collection.*

July 1, 1892. The "inadequate" cable ferry system continued to operate until its initial crossing.

It was rickety when I knew it. Probably more rickety now—but oh so beautiful! The High Wagon Bridge just invited one to explore. At age ten, taking my bike across the interstate bridge (with a tough uphill push) brought me down the other side to the Latsch Bathing Beach road, home of summertime fun and the remains of the old bridge. Whether out for a day of swimming at the beach or simply taking a bike hike to explore the wilds, I was in love with the space around that bridge.

We dived off the trail and ran down the river or crossed the old vestiges of the Wagon Bridge—fighting our way into the brambles of Wisconsin. We always stopped to peer through the cement balustrades at the easy flow of the Mississippi, thinking of the horses, wagons and early auto occupants crossing the bridge so many years ago on their way toward the High Bridge's river span to Winona.

JOHN'S GIFTS

John Latsch died in May 1909 of apparent "kidney trouble" at his family residence on Kansas and Wabasha Streets. He had been born on March 18, 1832. He deeded all of his property to the City of Winona. Since the business property had been taxed, son John A. soon increased the rent to himself to $6,000 per annum, to be paid to the city in lieu of taxes. The John Latsch Memorial Board, formed in February 1916, designated that money for the "poor fund." A referendum in 1934 asked Winona's voter permission to sell the business property and again add it to city tax rolls.

In the year 1916, the Scouts were given the Club House and grounds for use by Mr. Latsch, encompassing a former two-hundred-acre farm that was to form the new Prairie Island Park. In addition, the Boy Scouts Gamehaven Council was given a one-thousand-acre tract at Fountain City.

The Latsch Island (bathing beach) was traded for in 1917 in an exchange between the states of Minnesota and Wisconsin. An Act of Congress in 1918 confirmed the exchange of Pettibone Island at LaCrosse to Wisconsin and Latsch Island to Minnesota. Also, in 1917, John Latsch gave 47 acres to Winona for the Winona County Fairgrounds, adjacent to his previously donated West End Athletic Park. About 150 acres were earlier donated for East End parks.

In 1921, the City of Winona accepted Latsch's additional gift of eighty acres—twenty acres again destined for East End parks—"and the tract of land [sixty acres] immediately across the river—on either side of the dyke approach to bridge."

The popularity of the bathing beach in 1920 caused problems for city and bathhouse users. "Auto Parking Forbidden on Bridge" read the headlines. Apparently without a road into the island, parkers lined up for five hundred feet on the Wisconsin side bridge approach. They were told to "take bath house ferries or walk over the bridge." Yet in 1941, with the building of the new Interstate Bridge, there was still a search on by the city council, "seeking a road off the new bridge to the Latsch Island Beach." The state was to include a concrete step stairway down off the bridge on the Wisconsin side, but no road. Well remembered, we bounced our bikes down the long, extended steps to the lower road in the early 1950s. About that time, Mayor Floyd Simon proposed closing the beach and building a swimming pool in Winona proper.

There were some "showoffs" at the beach. In 1920, one of them, fully clothed salesman O.V. Olberg, hung off the old High Wagon Bridge adjacent to the original beach. O.V. climbed the bridge rails, teeter-tottered over the side and bathed fully clothed in the temperate waters until Winona police

The Latsch Bathing Beach served the multitudes for more than fifty years, succeeded by a Winona public swimming pool. *Courtesy Winona History Center.*

hauled him off to the hoosegow. Apparently, he had "imbibed in a bit too much hooch" before entertaining bathers. Other real, local high divers, like the Hicks boys, dived off the "springed," sixteen-foot tower and high dive with all manner of twists and turns.

SUPERINTENDENT S.T. BERTHE'S "PLEASURE island" of the 1920s had expert divers and swimmers, some of whom did "fancy diving" and "rode the breakers" on windy days. It also had a Beauty Contest, held there in 1926 as part of a Community Picnic to which all were invited. At the City Tourist Cabin grounds adjacent to the city Bathing Beach and Bathhouse on Latsch Island, box lunches were available and prizes were awarded to chosen "beauties." The pastor of the First Congregational Church was to speak after the 5:30 p.m. dinner.

The year 1926 also saw new booms installed at the John A. Latsch Public Bath Beach. The booms were made from timbers "of the old foot bridge across Lake Winona." The island's five tourist cabins were continued into the 1940s, with addition of a sixth cabin under the direction of caretaker Gerhardt McGill and WPA Parks representative Bill Hargesheimer in 1939.

We saw the high divers over all the years from our non-swimmer perches on the wooden "float" that enclosed us in a safe area. We were there to enjoy the "new foot of sand, the dredged swimming hole and the 72–76 degree water temperatures," as echoed by the *Republican-Herald*, on many of the days from June through August. From the start, there were thousands (twenty thousand per year) who utilized the bathing beach and associated cold-water showers. We were there on some of the Sundays when there were more than eight hundred people in attendance—and kids were charged a nickel for a locker.

The beach hours (1:00 p.m. to dark) were free to kids on all other days. If we showed up at 10:00 a.m. on certain days, lifeguards offered swimming lessons free of charge. There were even some ladies who helped the little ones build sand castles. Sometimes, impromptu volleyball and baseball games broke out on the large beach.

Over all the years up to 1923, there were no drownings at the bathing beach.

The year 1923 was the "record year of 21,378 users," as well as the year of shared concern for water quality and the overall bathing experience. "Continually worsening conditions" of stagnant water brought the suggestion to abandon the present location and move the bathhouse and all to the south side of the island, where the "current will ensure a constantly changing supply of water." Again, John A. Latsch paid for dredging, filling, moving and development costs.

In 1939, Gerhardt "Cappy" McGill announced that the renovated bathhouse was "in tip-top shape" and that a fresh foot of sand would open the season on seventy-six-degree water. He had replaced the rope lifelines beyond the float with chains. Cappy was in charge of beach and staff for many years, with brother Robert assisting as lifeguard. Cappy had announced that all were to "leave their dogs at home," due to complaints received and obvious health concerns.

There was restlessness in 1944 with the increased accidental drowning of children in Lake Winona without adequate supervision and the diminishment of the bathing beach usage due to high water and lack of accessibility. It was suggested that the bathing beach ("safe but not visited") should be abolished and a swimming pool established.

In March 1934, unmarried son John A. Latsch died at age seventy-three. He had followed his father's teachings and philanthropy. As noted in the Winona Research Project, John A. was known to have "worked with an industry no employee could match." With his father's teachings and his own industry, "in boyhood he had little time to play." As such, with his driving force, he "decided to give other boys (and grownups) the opportunity for full enjoyment in healthful living—a permanent place of recreation." Thus his lifetime gifts to the many.

The John A. Latsch State Park property to the north of today's Whitman Dam was created from his largesse, as was a large portion of Whitewater State Park. He was cited for having "created the bathhouse and bathing beach, city playgrounds, recreation centers, baseball parks and city parks."

In addition, thousands of acres of the U.S. Wildlife Refuge north of Winona to Fountain City were donated. The Upper Mississippi Wildlife and Fish Refuge runs from Wabasha to Rock Island totalling 130,000 acres. With headquarters in Winona, John Latsch contributed thousands of acres to the refuge.

The *Milwaukee Journal* of September 2, 1919, offered tribute and "a pretty compliment" to John Latsch for his Wisconsin gift of nine hundred acres:

> *The gift of Trempealeau Mt. to Wisconsin for a state park provokes two pleasant thoughts. The giver, Mr. John A. Latsch of Winona, Minn., in providing that surroundings dear to his memory shall become the possession of all the people of the state, has given them a treasure that man could not make, to be a perpetual beauty spot and pleasure ground.*

John Latsch donated thousands of acres for public use in the Upper Mississippi River Refuge and city and state parks of Minnesota and Wisconsin. *Courtesy Winona History Center.*

And Mr. Latsch has not asked that this gift bear his name. Instead he has requested that it be named for the first white explorer to reach Trempealeau Mt., Nicholas Perrot, who built a fort there some years before 1700. No other name could mean so much. No other monument could be so appropriate. Mr. Latsch might have asked that this gift bear his name, but he has shown that his motive was not a memorial to himself, but the wish that many others might enjoy the bit of nature dear to him as his boyhood home.

Upon the gift, the *Galesville Republican* declared, "Would there be more men like John A. Latsch."

Merrick State Park of one thousand acres and Idlewild Park were similarly donated in 1930, with "river frontage stretching from Fountain City to Buffalo." Namesake George B. Merrick was a Prescott, Wisconsin "river steamboat pilot, Civil War veteran, historian, author—and friend of fellow pilot Samuel Clemens (Mark Twain)." His books and articles are available at the Minnesota Historical Society.

The Latsch will of 1934 "established an unusual trust." The totality of John A.'s estate ($547,980) was granted to three trusted employees for a designated period. They were to supervise the accounts and gain only endowment income. The trust after twenty years then went "lock, stock and barrel" to Winona General Hospital (85 percent), Woodlawn Cemetery (10 percent) and the Margaret Simpson Home (5 percent). The Latsch business was functioning in 1931, 1941 and 1946 at 50 West Second Street. By 1957, it was gone.

John and his father were known to be stockholders of the First National Bank for more than fifty years. John lived sparingly at the family home at 276 East Wabasha Street, "occupying only a small part of the house." He never owned or drove a car. The property soon became the Park Lane Apartments, later utilized in part by Winona notables Oscar Naas (Springdale Dairy) and Edward Korpela (Winona Art teacher and musician with Hal Leonard Orchestra).

With all the family gifts and appurtenances, the Latsch Memorial Board was created in 1916 with the finest of Winona's leaders volunteering to serve—namely Messrs. Choate, Watkins, Siebrecht, Lucas, Youmans and others. By 1953, John Ambrosen had been named to the board, demonstrating the board's continuance. With J. Russell Smith, J.R. McConnon and others, the 1950s board continued the "rules of operation of Prairie Island Park" and gave a gift to the Westfield Golf Course, continuing the Latsch tradition of continuous giving and prudent supervision.

Max Conrad Sr. spoke for many in 1934 when he offered of John A.: "A sterling character—genial, friendly, generous to a fault." Frank Fugina, erstwhile riverboat captain and earlier owner of riverfront properties, sold to Latsch at "a reasonable price" in 1933 some of the acres in Township 108 for Prairie Island Park. Captain Fugina said that John was "kind of heart, quiet, and unassuming—with a genial smile and hearty handshake."

Fugina stated in "Ol' Man River," his weekly newspaper column of the 1950s, that with the gift of Prairie Island, Latsch had created "a vast recreational area where boys and girls could swim, camp and picnic unmolested." The Wisconsin Conservation Department also spoke of "the unselfish spirit of John Latsch" in its resolution of recognition.

In total, Fugina estimated that Latsch's land gifts amounted to about eighteen thousand acres—an area equivalent to today's Dallas–Fort Worth Airport, said to be the size of Rhode Island, at thirty square miles. Notable that Winona's thirty acres of "Flying Field" were donated to the city in 1919 by Mr. Latsch, as well as the city's first boat harbor.

Ever was John enterprising and compassionate toward the needy. In the Depression years of 1932–34, he had "10,000 cords of [fire] wood cut off the property of Prairie Island for city dependents" to heat their homes, according to the Winona Research Project. He replaced the trees with rows of pine forest plantings marveled at many years later by this writer.

C.D. Tearse, noted Winonan, spoke for those of us who used and felt the gifts as part of our lives growing up in Winona: "His thoughts turned always to the youth of tomorrow, the generations yet unborn, the people who would find their homes in this region in years to come. His generosity overshadowed everything else."

John A. truly loved his little Indian canoe. It took him into the nooks and inlets along the river that he and generations of others have enjoyed over all the years. This "greatest philanthropist that ever lived in the Mississippi Valley could have owned outboard motor and automobile, but chose not to do so. His canoe took him where he needed to go," as noted in the Winona Research Project. It was said of John A.: "His memory is cherished by all who knew him….He contributed of his Ability, and Means to its Advancement—and will be greatly missed."

The original John Latsch established the pattern. His long voyage from Switzerland; his service to a new country in the Civil War; his unselfish manner of aiding new grocers and the poor; his business acumen, leading to his son's creation of natural outlets for hunters, campers, hikers and

John had neither outboard motor nor automobile. He traversed his many land gifts via river and backwaters, paddling his own canoe. *Author's collection.*

John A. Latsch. "Would there
be more men like John A.
Latsch—that many others
might enjoy the bit of nature
dear to him." *Courtesy Winona
History Center.*

fishermen; and his deeply felt legacy by the many who yet today enjoy his
gifts are altogether more remarkable than that of any other Winonan. He
could rightly be called "Father of Winona"—and should be accordingly
acknowledged. His son continued and expanded the family tradition.

As the *Republican-Herald* noted in May 1915, "During his long, honorable
and successful career in this city, he had [built] better than he knew." He
was known to have "unswerving honesty, application to business, thrift and
sagacity." The gifts of the Latsches are "nearly inexpressible." They were
"given in the same blessed spirit of Abou ben Adhour—because he loved
his fellowmen. To them it is lovingly dedicated. His gifts are more enduring
than shafts of granite or monuments of marble."

One of the earliest explorers to observe the beauty of the lands surrounding
Winona was Lieutenant Zebulon Pike. He observed in September 1805 after
"ascending Sugar Loaf" in words that speak for us yet today:

We had a most sublime and beautiful prospect. At our right the mountains we passed in the morning and the prairie in the rear; like distant clouds the mountains of the Prairie le Cross. Under our feet and on our left the Mississippi, winding itself by numerous channels [and] *forming many islands—as far as the eye could embrace the scene. It was altogether a prospect so variegated and romantic that a man may scarcely expect to enjoy such a one, but twice or three in the course of his life.*

With thanks for the Latsch legacy.

Arms of Steel

Fifty members strong, Troop 5 of Madison School assembled in the heart of downtown Winona in front of the Woolworth Store on Third Street, as directed by the scoutmaster at our Monday night meeting. We had half-stepped and hustled in the early morning haze and humidity past the well-known landmarks of our steamy river valley town to get there well in advance, following the motto of Boy Scouts to "Be Prepared."

Ours is the largest of the troops, and we are the newest members. I am there to march as a full-fledged Boy Scout for the first time. The sensational Fourth of July Parade down Main Street is a high point of our summer. Lining up in the fashion of World War II veterans, we each take our places in ranks assigned by the scoutmaster.

I am so proud of my new Boy Scout shirt, the yellow official BSA kerchief and its knotted neckerchief slide holder to keep the kerchief in place. With BSA emblazoned over my right front pocket, I am truly in the form of the Boy Scouts I see pictured in *Boys' Life* magazine.

Since age eight or so, I have been a member of the Boy Scouts. With the blue Cub Scout shirt, I attended den meetings in the school neighborhood, learning my way through Fox and Wolf books that covered everything from astronomy to knot-tying. We had den meetings in the warm environment of Rich Johnson's house.

In his parents' oversized kitchen of their old Victorian house on one of the finest streets of Winona, we were led through the steps and techniques of scouting by Rich's mom. She was a wonderful teacher who guided us through baking, woodcarving and the study of the stars. Completing the steps to Webelos was our crowning achievement—the completion of pre-scouting rigors that allowed us into the full Boy Scout experience. Today was our first "official" appearance.

Waiting in our semi-straight lines, we readied for final assembly, inspection and inspiration. The scoutmaster announced that he was looking to the ranks of the "tenderfoots" for a trio of volunteers to carry the flags at the front of the troop. One was to carry the U.S. flag, another the Minnesota flag and the third the Boy Scout troop flag. I was thrilled to be chosen and outfitted with the leather strap and holder to become the carrier of the troop flag.

Imagine being at the head of the troop to march with the bands, floats, dignitaries and other scouts down the Main Street of town to arrive at the bandshell at Lake Winona for the program to honor our country, veterans and the birth of our country. To be in full uniform at the head of the pack was the greatest honor to which I had ever been selected. I had put on my school patrol belt for several years in elementary school and held the patrol flag daily and had been a strong Cub Scout member who earned the necessary "notches" of the scouting program, but I had never imagined that those experiences would allow me to lead and carry a flag of honor for the most distinguished troop in town on such a momentous day.

The scoutmaster reviewed for us the proper procedure of flag carrying to show highest respect for the American flag. It would lead the troop. The state and troop flags would be two steps behind. All flags were to be carried "aloft and free," never flat or horizontal. With instructions clearly in mind, the troop was called to attention. A salute to the flag was given, and the Pledge of Allegiance recited by all.

Rich was at the lead with the U.S. flag. Davey held the state flag as my partner in the second row. With the Harley-Davidson three-wheeled police motorcycle escort at the head of the parade, followed by the VFW Honor Guard and the high school band, the parade was in motion. We headed down Third Street, took a sharp left onto Main and set off through the throng of parade viewers lining the route for the next mile.

In blocks ahead I spotted neighbors, school friends and several of my teachers as I proudly held the flag at what I thought was just the right angle. They shouted greeting and encouragement, knowing that this was a special honor for me.

Having passed by the Winona State Teachers College at the midway point of our parade, we were well on our way to successful completion, with the lake park area only blocks ahead. We were holding our positions and marching in time with the band when we suddenly saw Rich, the U.S. flag carrier, veer off to the left of center.

As a "lefty," we knew that he had a tendency to favor everything to the left side. He seemed to always have a bit of a tilt to the left in his walk and posture, as if a heavy weight were in his left hand and he couldn't get upright. But we had never seen him take such a pronounced departure from normal. He was headed for the crowd at curbside! The flag was in the proper position, but his direction was askew.

The next thing I knew, Rich was directly in front of me, having made up the several yards between us, and now on a collision course. I was concerned for his safety, but also for the flag and our duty to hold the colors aloft. He was upright, but somehow drifting in his own world, right in front of me. Using quick Boy Scout action, I stepped aside of Rich, grabbed his left arm with my right and attempted to aim him toward the lake. By now the scoutmaster, who had been marching to the left side of the troop, moved up quickly to resolve the situation.

Boy Scouts of Cannon Falls, Minnesota, carrying the flags on Memorial Day, 2015. *Author's collection.*

Putting his arm around Rich, he rescued the flag and handed it to me, with quick instructions to keep the American flag to the right of the troop flag. I knew that I was now in the lead, with the dual responsibility of troop and country. Hardly without a beat missed, we had completed the unanticipated maneuver—now to the applause of the watching crowd. Rich was whisked to curbside and safety, where the scoutmaster and observers came to his aid.

As I marched forward, certain of my task and uncertain of my abilities, I felt a strong hand on my right shoulder. Marching next to me was my eldest brother, Frank, a senior member of the troop and a Life Scout, with ranking second only to the ultimate Eagle Scout. He quietly directed me to remove the troop flag from its holder, hand it to him and replace it with the U.S. flag. Once accomplished, I was to take over front and center with the "Stars and Stripes." He fell in to my former spot at left of center, a few paces behind me. I was now leading the total troop—and my big brother.

I must have shown arms of steel in that position of honor, for my flag never wavered, save for the slight breeze created by the brisk march in the morning sunshine. We completed the journey to the lake park, placed our flags in the fixed holders of the bandshell and enjoyed the festivities of the day. Rich was found to be okay, with a bit of heat stroke, coupled with the excitement of the assignment.

We had marched. We had brought honor to our troop and country. We were thrilled beyond belief. Oh what a glorious day to actually see the Scout slogan of "Do a Good Turn Daily" come into play.

Minnesota

"The State that Works"

Today we see new ethnic groups added to our equation of homeostasis. Languages and heritage may differ, but the created amalgam of the Hiawatha Valley bluff lands continues. From glazed ham loaf to spicy salsa to leavened bread to baked coon and beans, there's yet a welcome at every table.

—Kinder, Gentler Ways, *KOS, 2014*

The Germans, Poles, Irish and Swedes got us going on the path to equity in Minnesota. Somalians, Cambodians, Ghanaians, Mexicans, Ethiopians and others have since joined in. With everyone's contribution, Minnesota has evolved and continues to do so, leading the nation with a sense of fairness, mutual expectation and productivity.

Our mutual effort of shoveling out from snow banks in winter over all the years may be partial cause for being easy members of a combined melting pot in an otherwise frozen landscape. We work together. For residents new and old, Minnesota and Minnesotans have stood the test of time. We have recognized challenges to be faced and taken strides together to make Minnesota "The State that Works," as described in a *Time* magazine cover story of the 1970s.

In my home county of Winona and the Hiawatha Valley, people made for beautiful memories. In homes of city, hilltop or valley, they exercised mutual welcome to small and large spaces throughout all the years. Past experiences and travels have left beautiful memories for me. I like to wander through them

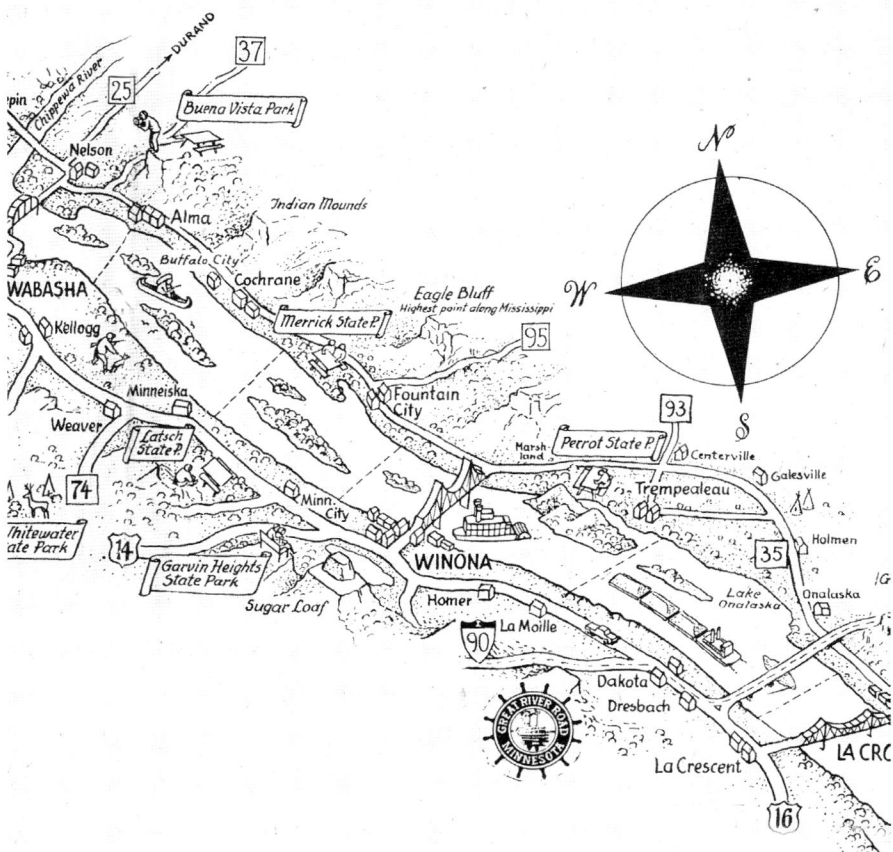

Above: Hiawatha Valley map depicting the start of the Great River Road, Highway 61, running from border to border (north–south). *Courtesy Winona History Center.*

Left: Highway 61, Red Wing. *Author's collection.*

Bluff scene, Red Wing/Lake City. *Author's collection.*

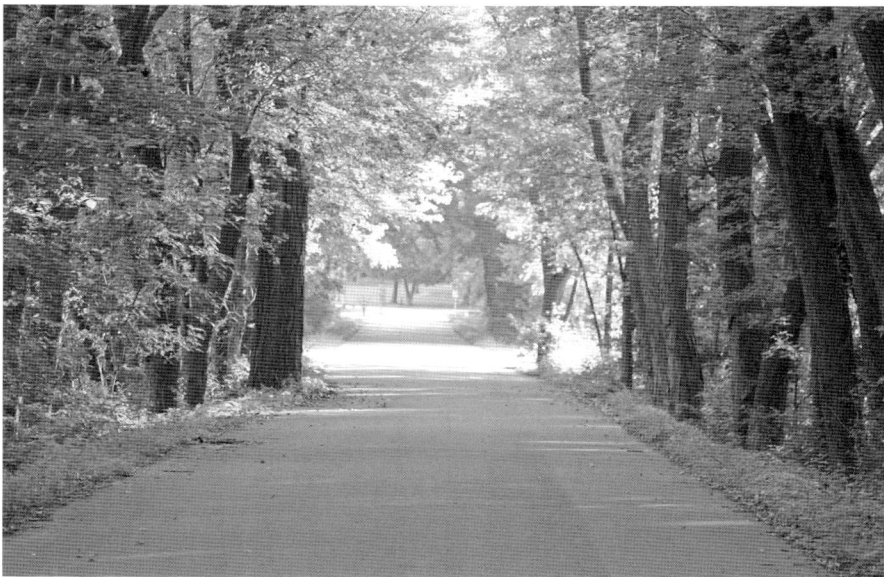

A trip through the Red Wing and Lake City area, with a stop at the Hok-Si-La Park entrance of Lake City on Lake Pepin. *Author's collection.*

all, thrilled to have met all the generations and many of the representative groups of the valley. They have created a lifetime of memories. Continued research affirms those remembrances.

A CHANCE TO GROW

This story gives simple evidence of three-quarters of a century of homegrown life in a state that allowed one Minnesotan the chance to find his way into the workforce and society. With a sense of equity tucked in his back pocket and the larger world inviting, he made his steps. Alongside the poor and the rich, the educated and the not so, this observer competed.

Today, he gives high marks to the people of Minnesota for imbuing a sense of fairness and sharing. In his lifetime, he was offered opportunity to risk, to challenge and to expand his psyche and experiences throughout life. No one stood in his way. Playing alongside others across the state from the elementary school basketball court into graduate school research some few years later, he held his own.

A few he met along the way became millionaires and titans. They found their satisfaction by later giving back to the community. Many of his peers from similarly challenged backgrounds became teachers, authors, researchers and societal determiners. Insight gained in the journey led this writer to a lifetime of pride and satisfaction of being one who loves his Minnesota, his "flyover land."

It didn't just happen that he had every opportunity. Some led and risked before him to establish the forms of gumption, grit and giving that characterizes his fellow Minnesotans.

A SHARED HISTORY

By AD 800, wild rice had become a staple crop in northern Minnesota for indigenous residents, with corn (maize) establishing itself farther south. In the next few hundred years, the Mississippian culture of the north reached into the southeast portion of the present state to form large Native American villages, including Keoxa (Wah-Pa-Sha's Prairie), later to be called Winona, the author's hometown.

Artist's depiction of Keoxa/Wapasha's Prairie (Winona, Minnesota). *Courtesy Winona History Center.*

The Mississippian culture of early times may have been precursor and motivator to the people of Minnesota. A Dakota Native American culture descended from peoples of the Mississippian culture; this first laboratory of social inequality may have motivated future generations of Minnesotans toward equity for all.

Even in earliest cultures, social inequality occurred. When resources of a given society are distributed unevenly, typically through norms of allocation, there become specific patterns along lines of socially defined categories of persons. In tribal societies, a tribal head or chieftain held some privileges, used some tools or wore marks of office to which others did not have access.

Social inequality is found in almost every society. In simple societies, social inequality may have been very low, with few social roles and statuses occupied by its members. But as a boy without means in a later century of Minnesota, it felt as if opportunity was there to grow in all directions, even though there were known variables of economics unevenly distributed. If one were to achieve those gains, it was readily apparent that one had to do it the old-fashioned way, by earning it.

The state of Minnesota was shaped by Native American origins, by European exploration and settlement and by the emergence of industries made possible by the state's natural resources. Minnesota achieved prominence through fur trading, logging and farming, later to become known for railroads and iron mining.

When Europeans first started exploring Minnesota, the region was inhabited primarily by tribes of Dakotas, with the Ojibwas (sometimes called Chippewas or Anishinaabes) beginning to migrate westward into the state around 1700. The economies of these tribes were chiefly based on hunter-gatherer activities. The French were dominant in their early exploration of the region and left their mark, with names of Trempealeau, Perrot, LeSeur and Hennepin. Explorer LeSeur designated the Indian sand prairie village of Keoxah "la Prairie aux Ailes" ("Wing's Prairie") in 1701.

The Homestead Act in 1862 facilitated land claims by settlers on land both cheap and fertile. Railroads to serve industry and farms to serve the nation were built out in Minnesota. Led by the Northern Pacific Railway and the St. Paul and Pacific Railroad, the railroad industry advertised the opportunities in the state and worked to get immigrants to settle in Minnesota, often on large swaths of railroad right-of-way. The Winona and St. Peter Railroad extended itself to Minnesota's western border and beyond.

After the Civil War, Minnesota became an attractive region for European immigration and settlement. Minnesota's population in 1870 was 439,000; the number would triple during two subsequent decades. Settlement occurred with thousands of laborers coming from the eastern states and Europe to feed the new industrial machines of mining, railroading, sawmilling and flour making.

MINNESOTA IN ACTION

The economy of Minnesota is now driven by banking, computers, manufacturing and healthcare, although early natural industries remain important. The Mayo Clinic, with forty thousand employees in Minnesota, is the largest employee in the state. With outlet hubs in Arizona, Florida, Georgia, Iowa and Wisconsin and more than sixty thousand employees committed to excellence of care, Mayo's revenues for 2018 surpassed $12 billion.

General Mills and Cargill participate wholly in today's world markets. They started in the 1800s to lead us down the river and across railway paths, with grain, corn and the manufactured flour leaving from mills of Stillwater,

Minneapolis and Winona. The formation of WCCO Radio of Minneapolis in 1938 occurred as the Washburn Company's (WC) early communicator of market grain and corn prices to farmers.

The recent merger of Spam and Skippy Peanut Butter and a new natural foods product line at Hormel of Austin brings to the world a smorgasbord of meal options for the consumer. One can only extrapolate the permutations and combinations of peanut butter and Spam and natural foods to choose for the evening meal.

Winona's Wincraft satisfies the prize needs, banners and the like for the Super Bowl, NFL, National Hockey League and a world market well beyond the limestone hills of southern Minnesota. Its 1960s contracts with the major leagues made them world leaders from its humble start on West Fifth Street. Hal Leonard of east Winona and Second Street serves as the world's leader in the print music market (now out of New York). Fastenal's $5 billion of annual sales originated in a small shop just off Second Street. Accordingly, Minnesota was named by CNBC the "No. 1 State in the Nation for Business" in June 2015.

Today, there is a balanced mix of agriculture and manufacturing in cities like Rochester, Minneapolis and St. Paul. Forestry and mining have diminished over the years, with agriculture holding its own. Manufacturing of cement trucks and computers and heart implant devices has led Minnesota into world markets. Our corn and soybeans ship out of the state and country. Our lumberjacks have been replaced in the north by tourism and by a strong relatedness to the North Dakota oil market boom.

World leaders seem to find their way to small, rural southeastern Minnesota towns via the Mayo Clinic of Rochester, and they learn to stay. Rochester is presently on the cusp of merging with the metropolitan area through unbelievable growth of city and nearby, transformed cornfields.

Neighboring Wisconsin and Minnesota have been "two peas in a pod" over the past one hundred years. June has always been "Dairy Month" in both states. Minnesota has recently ceased being a mirror image to its Mississippi River bordered neighbor, however, now outdistancing them. The trend is clear when we look at the populations of Minneapolis–St. Paul and Milwaukee. The Twin Cities population now approaches 3.5 million people, contrasted to Milwaukee's 1.5 million.

The *Minneapolis Star Tribune* reported on March 8, 2015:

> *When you put critical mass of business, academic and government together, you get "a stew of ideas" that is greater than the sum of its parts.*

Accordingly since the late 1960s, income per capita has made Minnesota "an upper-income state" and Wisconsin "below average."

Minnesota has the stew—my "Mulligan mix"—that says, correspondingly, that Minnesotans are healthier—and more of them go on to college—66% vs. 59%.

The Gophers have overtaken the Badgers.

THOSE WHO MADE A DIFFERENCE

Early founders of our state in the late 1800s were gentrified, proper and rugged individualists. Although some became railroad tycoons and wealthy millers, they established a culture of egalitarianism. Minnesota belonged to all. More recent homegrown leaders brought the frosting to the cake.

Governor Floyd Olson was "a hero of the local labor unions." With three terms in office in the 1930s, he is consistently considered one of the greatest governors in Minnesota history and one of the most influential American politicians of his era.

During his tenure, formerly quiet labor unions began asserting themselves rather forcefully. The Minneapolis Teamsters Strike of 1934 turned ugly, with the union demanding the right to speak for all trucking employees. As a result of Olson's leadership through this strike and many others that followed across the nation, Congress passed the National Labor Relations Act of 1935.

Harold Stassen, "boy governor of Minnesota" (1939–43), was an up-and-coming candidate who gave the keynote speech at the Republican National Convention of 1940. His father, a German/Czech farmer, was often elected mayor of West St. Paul—a good model for young Harold. Harold made a difference.

Populist governor, World War II U.S. Marine and wounded war hero Major Orville Freeman delivered the nomination speech for John F. Kennedy at the Democrat National Convention of 1960. Freeman represented the people for years, later serving as U.S. Secretary of Agriculture until 1969. A personal picture taken with this governor as a part of our boyhood School Patrol visitation to the state capitol in 1955 was a highlight of this writer's youth.

Hubert Humphrey, Minneapolis mayor and U.S. senator for a twenty-year period in the 1950s and '60s, was largely responsible for the Civil

Left: Hubert Horatio Humphrey, Minnesota U.S. senator, 1949–64 and 1971–78, and thirty-eighth vice-president of the United States, 1964–68. *Courtesy U.S. Senate Historical Office, used with permission.*

Right: Eugene McCarthy, Minnesota U.S. representative, 1949–59, and Minnesota U.S. senator, 1959–71. *Courtesy U.S. Senate Historical Office, used with permission.*

Rights Act of 1964. I was proud to see him as he stood on the second-floor platform at the world's first indoor shopping center, Southdale of Edina, and absolutely beamed his message with strength and commitment and sincerity. He touched our hearts and stayed with us for many years.

Addressing the 1948 Democratic National Convention in Philadelphia, Hubert delivered a "fiery, impassioned speech" urging delegates to include a civil rights plank in the Democratic platform, stating in part: "There are those who say to you we are rushing this issue of civil rights. I say we are 172 years late….The time has arrived for the Democratic Party to get out of the shadow of states' rights and walk forthrightly into the bright sunshine of human rights." His son "Skip" continued the family tradition.

Senator Eugene McCarthy—governor, congressman, senator and presidential candidate from 1949 to 1971—was a national force in the Democrat Party. A poet and antiwar advocate, McCarthy had roots in Watkins, Minnesota, where he was "a bright student who spent hours reading his aunt's Harvard Classics." He was deeply influenced by the monks at nearby St. John's Abbey and University, where he spent nine months as a novice before he left the monastery, causing a fellow novice to say, "It was like losing a twenty-game [baseball] winner."

Born on a farm in South Dakota to Norwegian parents, U.S. Senator Edward Thye (1943–59) represented our rights. His brother, Ted, became a professional wrestler in the Great Northwest—another bastion of the "good guy" winning out, as we saw on Saturday night "rassling" in the Red Men's Wigwam of the 1940s and '50s.

So very many Minnesotans were self-made men and women. They were leaders and equal-opportunity models for those of us growing up in the classrooms of Minnesota. With pictures of Washington and Lincoln looking down on us, our female elementary and high school teachers gave us strength. Milkmen, bakers, truck drivers, farmers, lawyers, police officers, ministers and storeowners watched over us as we grew. At home, my grandfather and father were reelected as local leaders of union teamsters and craftsmen from the 1900s into the fiery 1930s.

LIFE AT HOME

Politics weren't discussed in our home, although there were often loud and challenging words about unions between Pa and older brothers. Some of the five boys at home heard the line from a frustrated father, who said, "All I have about me is a bunch of educated bums." We all found our own way into college, the military or other non-union vocations—not becoming Pa's favored carpenter or bricklayer. One of us was a steady, summer dump truck driver with a union badge and chauffeur's button on his hat, however. I was proud of Pa's leadership and the union's achievements in getting drivers like me a steady, strong wage (and time-and-a-half after forty hours) to pay my way through the local teacher's college.

We didn't have an attorney in the family or we may have each followed the Stassen or Humphrey or Freeman model. Pa was our leader. He was always pleased to receive a Christmas card from Senator Ed Thye, whom he knew through Winona labor leadership and actions. In May 1948, Thye was called a national "housing leader" for his stance on low-cost housing for all Americans. In 1954, speaking to Minnesota elementary school children, he suggested, "I am sure that each of you will agree with

Left: Wendell Anderson, governor of Minnesota, 1971–76, and Minnesota U.S. senator, 1976–78. *Courtesy U.S. Senate Historical Office, used with permission.*

Right: Edward Thye, governor of Minnesota, 1943–47, and Minnesota U.S. senator, 1947–59. *Courtesy U.S. Senate Historical Office, used with permission.*

me that you are indeed fortunate to be living in a nation based upon democratic principles, where each adult citizen has the right, and indeed the responsibility, of expressing himself in the affairs of his government." We were fortunate.

Pa didn't live to see his five boys with ten college degrees, two earning highest noncommissioned officer status and decoration in the USAF over forty cumulative years, and the nearly sixty-five years of service to education and community by others, including one who occasionally shared a stage or two with a Minnesota senator or governor.

We each "expressed ourselves" as we grew. Sadly, two of the boys were gone by age forty or so. But freedom had been ours to achieve. Little sister did her part by supporting all the boys throughout life and by making her own contributions to church and community, including her recent, donated million-dollar property to a rural county in Wisconsin for a wild and natural park—focusing on bluebirds and serenity.

Folks like Vice President Walter Mondale and Governor Jesse Ventura all left an impression on the people. Governor Wendell Anderson, an

Olympic hockey player and scholar, created "the Minnesota Miracle" of equity in taxes and school funding in 1970. At the local level, we saw judges, school officials and police who represented the populace and held us all to account. We understood the limits of "good" and "fair," as well as the concomitant expectations.

RESPONSIBILITY FOR TODAY

From world peace to massive electric transmission lines to exported grain prices and continuous protection of "North Star State" natural resources, our Minnesota leaders continue to express themselves. Significant inequalities in income and wealth yet exist when specific, socially defined categories of people are compared. Among the most pervasive of these are sex/gender, race and ethnicity.

My observation suggests that income level has been a significant social delimiter. Some with greater dollars have tried to make the world their domain (and still attempt to do so). Yet the common man or woman can overcome these issues. In Minnesota, merit is considered to be a primary factor determining one's place or rank in the social order. Merit and commitment can have effects on variations in income, wealth or social status.

My experience suggests that it is simply to be earned. No one will give you the merits or treasures of society unless you take personal responsibility for earning them. One simply goes to work and continuously outworks the other. Gender, race and ethnicity have nothing to do with it.

When teaching a class in the University of Minnesota's Graduate School of Education, this lecturer was assigned a classroom in the prestigious Science/Engineering Building of the campus. Posted therein was a bulletin board of names and pictures of professors and graduate school students in engineering, many of whom were seeking a PhD. The grand majority of posted pictures were of foreign-born students and professors. Absent were the smiling faces of hometown Minnesota young adults.

Even at the beginning university level, there is a significant shift of student enrollment from a former male-dominated to a female-dominated population. The Pew Research Center (2014) reports that enrollment of recent high school graduates in college in 1994 was in the low 60th percentiles for male and female alike. Today, women outpace men in

The American flag stands proudly on Minnesota's shores throughout every season. *Author's collection.*

enrollment by at least 10 percentage points, with some races as high as 15 percentage points higher.

As much as we hate to give up our natural environment, we have allowed Texas companies and others to haul it away. They have discovered that limestone bluff "frac sand" of southern Minnesota is to their liking in the booming gas and oil production environments. Virtually every village on both sides of the Mississippi has been touched by the "frac sand" machine. It is shipped night and day out of state via barge lines from Winona and Wabasha to a host of downriver states—right past the front door of the homegrown, nineteen-thousand-employee Fastenal Company that originated in Winona.

Fastenal of Winona is fast becoming the world's largest supplier of nuts and bolts to industry through more than 2,500 stores and billions of dollars of sales. 3M of St. Paul leads the world in production of abrasive products. Honeywell, Control Data and some of the early computer related industries have been subsumed and replaced by multitudes of new suppliers needing an ever more skilled workforce. Disk drives are made in Bloomington.

Author's collection.

Author's collection.

From the southern shoreline through the river valley and on to a grand north country of tamaracks, open pit mines and ten thousand lakes, Minnesota's natural treasures abound. *Author's collection.*

The unemployment rate of Minnesota is the nation's lowest. Skilled workers are in demand. Shutterfly and Amazon have come to Shakopee. Medical insurance companies continue to merge hand over fist and center themselves in the ever-growing metro area. We're world headquarters to Dairy Queen, Target and Polaris. Toyota and others continue to gain President Award Citations for their exemplary auto dealerships in our state.

There are yet issues to be sorted out. Minnesota continues to put a high priority on education at all levels, often leading the nation with test scores, although metro schools do poorly on all testing. We need another "Minnesota Miracle." The abundance of local referendums has caused severe inequity in school fund allocation across the state. There is entitlement in certain districts and woeful loss in the majority of other districts.

"Right to work" legislation is fast becoming a hot issue, with neighbor Wisconsin's recent passing of the same. Effectively, this corporate-sponsored legislation will deflate the effectiveness of labor unions and the workingman.

We need again the "common man"—a Floyd Olson, Edward Thye, Al Quie or Wendell Anderson—to step out from the populace and exert his or her significant human power. The future of Minnesota depends on those who can use a hockey stick as well as complete a law degree. We need our young ladies and gentlemen of all nationalities to assert their considerable strengths to protect the beauty of life and fairness of Minnesota's future.

There are no excuses—only opportunity in "the state that works."

Bibliography

Bunnell, Lafayette Houghton, MD. *Winona (We-no-na) and Its Environs on the Mississippi in Ancient and Modern Days*. N.p.: Jones & Kroeger, 1897. Personal copy.

Clemens, Samuel. *Mark Twain: The Adventures of Tom Sawyer*. N.p., 1876. Personal copy, 1992 edition.

Hughes, Thomas. *Indian Chiefs of Southern Minnesota, 1825–1865*. Minneapolis, MN: Ross & Haines, 1969. Personal copy.

Longfellow, Henry Wadsworth. *The Song of Hiawatha*. London: Everyman, 1992. First published in 1855. Personal copy.

Nilles, Myron A. *A History of Wapasha's Prairie, 1660–1853*. Winona, MN: Winona County Historical Society, 2005. Personal copy.

U.S. Senate Historical Office. Personal contact and approval.

Williamson, John P., AM, DD. *An English-Dakota Dictionary: Wasicun Ka Dakota Ieska Wowapi*. New York: American Tract Society, 1902. Personal copy.

Winona City Directories. Winona Public Library. Continuous personal research over forty-year period of residences, people and locations. Personal copies (5).

Winona County Historical Society. *History of Winona County*. Chicago: H.H. Hill and Company, 1883. Reprint, 1977. Personal copy.

Winona History Center, 2018. Personal research and assistance of archivists.

Winona Newspaper Project/Winona State University. Online database of one hundred years of local newspapers. Utilized consistently for ten years of research, verification and support.

About the Author

Kent Stever has spent a lifetime in and about the Hiawatha Valley. Enjoying the remembrances and feelings of a life well lived in one of the nation's most scenic areas, he has authored numerous articles and four nonfiction books, reflected on from his lakeside home in Lakeville, Minnesota. With more than fifty years as teacher, principal, Dale Carnegie leader and university lecturer, his in-depth research identifies growth of the region and patterns of society.

Testimony to felt love, joy and depth of growing up in a river town of the Hiawatha Valley is enhanced through personal vignettes. "He lived what he learned."

Visit us at
www.historypress.com
···